Member Stories

2007

Sexaholics Anonymous
International Central Office
P. O. Box 3565, Brentwood, TN 37024-3565
Phone: 615-370-6062
Toll Free: 866-424-8777
Fax: 615-370-0882
Website: www.sa.org
E-Mail: saico@sa.org

SA Statement of Principle

We have a solution. We don't claim it's for everybody, but for us, it works. If you identify with us and think you may share our problem, we'd like to share our solution with you (Sexaholics Anonymous, last sentence, page 2).

In defining sobriety, we do not speak for those outside Sexaholics Anonymous. We can only speak for ourselves. Thus, for the married sexaholic, sexual sobriety means having no form of sex with self or with persons other than the spouse. In SA's sobriety definition, the term "spouse" refers to one's partner in a marriage between a man and a woman. For the unmarried sexaholic, sexual sobriety means freedom from sex of any kind. And for all of us, single and married alike, sexual sobriety also includes progressive victory over lust (Sexaholics Anonymous, 191-192).

The only requirement for SA membership is a desire to stop lusting and become sexually sober according to the SA sobriety definition.

Any two or more sexaholics gathered together for SA sobriety according to SA sobriety definition may call themselves an SA group.

Meetings that do not adhere to and follow Sexaholics Anonymous' sobriety statement as set forth in the foregoing Statement of Principle adopted by the General Delegate Assembly in 2010 are not SA meetings and shall not call themselves SA meetings.

Addendum to the Statement of Principle passed by the General Delegate Assembly on July 8, 2016.

Responsibility Statement

I am responsible. When anyone, anywhere reaches out for help,
I want the hand of SA always to be there. And for that: I am responsible.

ISBN 0-9755986-0-0

Preface

This collection of thirty-five recovery stories was written by members of Sexaholics Anonymous (SA) over a period of years beginning in the 1980s. Generally, they tell what it was like living in addiction to lust, what happened to change that course, and what it is like living in sobriety and recovery. Some of the stories are new, but most appeared previously, either in *Member Stories 1989* or in *Essay*, the fellowship's newsletter. Many have undergone revisions by the authors based on feedback and suggestions by editors and other SA members. They provide a sampling of fellowship recovery to date.

This volume reflects years of work by members of Sexaholics Anonymous. We offer it in gratitude to the fellowship and to all those seeking recovery from lust addiction.

These [personal stories] give a fair cross section of our membership and a clear-cut idea of what has actually happened in their lives.

We hope no one will consider these self-revealing accounts in bad taste. Our hope is that many [sexaholic] men and women, desperately in need, will see these pages, and we believe that it is only by fully disclosing ourselves and our problems that they will be persuaded to say, "Yes, I am one of them too; I must have this thing."

—Alcoholics Anonymous 29

Table of Contents

1. I'm a Sexaholic

"I'm a sexaholic." I can still remember the first time I said that at an SA meeting. My palms were sweaty, my heart was pounding, my throat had a lump in it, and I could hardly speak—pretty much the same reaction I used to get each time I approached a prostitute or practiced any of my other addictive sexual behaviors.

Before SA my life was full of those powerless episodes when "something" would come over me. My ritual would begin, and I would end up doing the same things I had said over and over that I would never again do. How many times had I said, "Never again"? Whether it was going to prostitutes several times a week, spending hours in a porno arcade, or masturbating ten times a day, my life was constantly filled with sexual fantasy and lust. It seems my every thought was about sex. Every woman who walked past was a lust object. When I was driving, I was always looking into the car next to me or scanning the sidewalk for something or someone to feed my lust, someone or something to help me escape from the real world.

I somehow allowed this sexual addiction (although I didn't know to call it that at the time) to control and destroy my life. I could never get enough. I was always searching for the perfect fix, the right connection. I continually crossed my boundaries. I would tell myself that I'd never do this or that, but sooner or later I would. So I'd draw a new line; then I'd cross that one too. Who knows where the lines would have ended?

I spent countless dollars and hours on this terrible addiction. I lied to my family, my friends, and my employers. I lost jobs, I lost one marriage, and I was in the midst of destroying another family (and they didn't even know what was happening!). I had been beaten up by pimps, I had contracted diseases, and I had lost all self-esteem. I felt that I was the lowest scum on earth. I knew that if anyone knew the real me, they would be disgusted and I would be forever humiliated. But none of this made me stop. Nothing I tried seemed able to make me stop or to make the need go away.

I tried will power, will power, and more will power. I tried psychotherapy. I tried group therapy. I tried hypnosis. I tried religion. I tried New Age spirituality. I tried getting divorced. I tried getting remarried. I tried doing it over and over again until I got sick of it. I tried more and more will power.

All I got was more guilt, more shame, more self-doubt, more fuel for that ever-increasing downward spiral. Absolutely nothing worked—nothing. I didn't know where to go, to whom to turn. I was so alone, so ashamed, and so afraid–until I found SA. Then my life was turned around.

It was not easy at the beginning. When I got sober, in 1986, I went through terrible withdrawal symptoms, both physical and emotional. I was mad at the world, I felt sorry for myself, I was continually exhausted, I was bombarded by even more lustful thoughts. But, after about two months, it did get easier. The impossible became possible.

I didn't think it was humanly possible never to masturbate again. But I found that, contrary to my addictive thinking, the longer I went without, the easier it got. I found that, far from quenching my lustful desires, masturbation had actually been fueling them.

The darkness, the fear, the shame, the isolation, and the slavery to my addiction are gone. The addiction is still there; it will always be there. But it no longer has mastery over me and my life. There is no "other" me that has to hide in the shadows; no dark side that has to escape the shame and guilt of its disgusting behavior by doing that same behavior over and over again.

Instead, there is simply me. I'm still recovering and far from perfect. But the one I see in the mirror and the one the world sees are now one and the same. What a wonderful gift, to be one person instead of two—more freeing and joyful than I ever dreamed possible. Not only that, but as long as I continue to work the Twelve Steps of Sexaholics Anonymous, I am able to pass this gift along to others. What a blessing! What a miracle!

I can still remember the chills that went down my spine as I listened at my first SA meeting. These men and women were telling *my* story, and they had never met me before. They had been through it. They had the same problem I did. They knew the shame and guilt. They understood the powerlessness. *But they were in recovery.* I never dreamed there were people who could share this nightmare, and I never dreamed that I would find a whole room full of people who were recovering from it. I thought I was going to be trapped in that desolate isolation and addiction forever. I thought I would die in it.

The fellowship and understanding were just the beginning. There were tools I could learn to use for my recovery, tools which would help end the diabolical domination my addiction had over me. I learned how to avoid the triggers which seemed to start my acting out rituals. I learned to surrender the lust and the urges. I learned to use the telephone to call my friends in SA when things started to get bad, or when things were good, or when things just *were*. Most of all, I learned to work SA's Twelve Steps of recovery.

And I do mean *work*. I worked harder at my recovery from the domination of this crippling disease than I had ever worked at anything in my entire life. And I continue to work diligently at my recovery every day of my life. But the payoff has been a thousand times more than I ever dreamed possible.

I thank God that I was at such a low bottom when I found this program. Had I not already tried everything else, had I not been at my wit's end, I don't know if I could have accepted all that SA has to offer, or that I would have been willing to work so hard in the Twelve Step program. I might have been my usual, scoffing self. Fortunately, this bottom allowed me to accept my powerlessness. It allowed me to trust in those who had walked the same path to recovery before me. It allowed me to find a Power greater than myself whom I could trust to lead me to sanity. It enabled me to turn my whole life around—my *whole* life, not just the sexaholic part.

2. A Curious Kid

I was a curious girl, born into a family where I learned a lot about power and control, but nothing about intimacy. Sometimes I'd sneak around our house, looking for clues about my family. When I was seven, I found pictures of nudes in art books and men's magazines under my father's bed. Although my first reaction was disgust, "looking" soon became an obsession. For the next ten years, I knew where to go to get an instant mood alteration. For sexaholics this is called the allergy and the mental obsession. I told none of my friends about this; this was mine alone.

As a teenage sexaholic I found that although others were curious about sex and lust, not everyone wanted intrigue. I did—and quickly developed the sexaholic radar that spots others with vulnerability to this interest. They were not always the nicest, most honest, or most stable people in my crowd. I had an illusion about my own virtue and maintained a double standard easily. License to act out guided most of my decisions. Friends wondered how I could live with myself because I would dump one date who didn't want to have sex for another who did. "Lighten up," I'd laugh. I was a fun-loving searcher. I was free!

I thought I was free, but this behavior held back the development of social and intimacy skills. When I arrived at SA in my thirties I was still psychologically under the bed, alone with my father's pictures.

When did this "freedom" become slavery? I got involved in many incidents that shocked me: seducing the fourteen-year-old brother of a college friend when my target of choice said no; sex with a cousin on a family visit; sex with a brother's best friend; fondling a baby I was babysitting in college; obsession with certain animals. My lust had no limits.

At nineteen I was told about masturbation by a dorm mate. I saw how convenient it was. No more having to flirt until someone was interested. I could fantasize on my own schedule. I chose to have fewer friends; they might get in my way if masturbation or a "relationship" called.

I married in my twenties when I found a man whom I could flatter and who was willing to give sex on demand. Unfortunately, marriage didn't cure my sexaholism. I craved lust, and my spouse came to resent being treated as an object. I missed the intrigue. I began flirting around the edges of my marriage, with friends' husbands, friends of my husband, people at work. Soon I had to masturbate to enjoy sex with my spouse at all. I denied that there was anything wrong with me. I started to build a case against my spouse. I belittled him and told him what a disappointment he was to me. It wasn't long until I found someone at work who was willing to fall into lust with me. One new partner led to another. My marriage was now exposed as a relationship I couldn't let go of, or get lust out of.

In my thirties I needed more and different sensations: to be in love, in pain, in intrigue, and to masturbate chronically. Rejections, which were inevitable, left me in suicidal states, which seemed to add to the high. I would brood, think of killing others and myself, cry, rage, threaten, and stalk. I don't know if I was angry because people dared to withhold the drug from me, or if I enjoyed the aftershocks.

Many unmanageable years followed, which included an abortion, being found out at work, the risk of HIV, and several painful rejections. I vowed to stop all my foolishness. I retreated to masturbation and a civil, but sexless, relationship, living with my spouse as my roommate. This period of control lasted several years with the use of cruel, sadistic masturbation fantasies. I wanted to escape. I got the bright idea of taking a trip to the other side of the world alone. I told myself it was a spiritual search: actually, I wanted to see if sex on the other side of the world might cure me.

This trip was dangerous, humiliating, and expensive. On my return, I found I could not turn off my lust. I played "kneesies" with strangers on buses. I gave pornography to teenaged nephews as Christmas presents. I took hits on the street compulsively and unmanageably.

Fear motivated me to seek help. I started reading self-help books and listening to recovery tapes. Finally, reading a bulletin board in a church one day, I learned about SA. I knew when I heard my first share that I was home. However, it took me a year of regular meetings to surrender my "right" to masturbate. After my last slip, when I feebly laughed and reported it to the group, I saw in their faces only pity and compassion. I realized then that, unless I seized upon the program they were offering, I was a loser going nowhere. That day in 1992 I surrendered completely, and I have been sober since then.

Married sexaholics new to the program are often surprised to hear that the abstinence contract in my marriage lasted four and a half years, but that's what it took. When we met, I was an active sexaholic. Our early knowledge of each other (or at least mine of him) was sexually based. His childhood religion was different from mine. I barely noticed anything about his character and personality. My father had told me years before that what kept people together was physical, and I believed it. This was the most damaging idea I held on to. I had to discard it. When I got sober, I didn't know who we were without lust.

I love the old-timer who said that his great spiritual awakening came when he gave his wife the towel rack nearest to the sink. My husband knew I was dishonest, lazy, selfish, and thoughtless. Our great breakthrough came when he asked me to start saying good morning to him every day.

"Every morning?" I asked.

"One day at a time," he replied.

From that beginning, we have built a spiritual foundation which has begun to cement us in a way we had never experienced before.

When I was newly sober, I grieved for my lust. It had been my only real relationship. I loathed hugs or anything "corny" from my spouse. Now we are sincerely interested in each other. We can hold hands, cuddle, and hug to express our love—not because I'm feeling needy.

The abstinence contract that our literature recommends has allowed us to recover from lust on both sides of the marriage. We spend time in "no crosstalk" sharing. Three minutes become five, and then ten. Now, with the help of the fellowship, we have established the spiritual foundation that must come before physical touch for me as a recovering sexaholic.

Service in SA is the best way for me to get to know other people. By giving of myself, I have learned to find out what the other guy thinks and feels and the joy of working together for common interests. I have learned boundaries and commitment and that it is forgivable to make mistakes. A sponsee of mine lost $200.00 from the intergroup's treasury recently. I told her she would not be asked to step down, and she wasn't. She found it in her closet a week later.

Control isn't pretty, and I'd rather admit to it in meetings with other control freaks who are learning to let go. I do not want to have to learn about letting go on the job, in a new relationship, or in a church group. I saw that the people in the program who give really do reap the greatest rewards. I was advised not to hold back as too shy, controlling, or nervous. I was told to take a job I need to learn how to do. Even if I fail, my group will love me and support me. Service works for me.

It is my belief that my sexaholic mind cannot heal itself. In any given week, my group may include a minister in recovery, a tennis pro, a retired beautician, a young divorcee, and a husband trying to hold on to his angry wife or family. Not one of them is any different from the next. We all have heads full of fantasy and dependency relationships and require the new pair of glasses that AA speaks about. The ones among us who decide to alter their lusting by half measures fall by the wayside. I have seen it happen time and again.

The Big Book of AA says that half measures availed us nothing. I was sick and tired of lust ruining my life. I had to surrender my right to it once and for all with no conditions. I began lusting before my brain was fully logical. It was a shock to grasp that lust was not somehow essential in order for me to be me! I now know that lust twisted my life and prevented my Higher Power from using me to help others. When I remember this, I would not trade my worst day of sobriety for my best day of lust. I am resolved to hang on to my sobriety no matter what, to stay involved in the program, and to feed my spiritual side. I know God will do the rest.

3. It Couldn't Happen to Me

"You have the right to remain silent," the officer said as he placed the cold chrome bracelets around my wrists. I couldn't believe this was actually happening to me. I had a reputation as a solid moral citizen and was well respected in my community, but now I was under arrest. It had to be just a bad dream—but no, this devastating thing was happening to me!

My father came from a family of alcoholics and had problems with alcohol throughout his life, but only after I reached my teens did his behavior affect me to a great degree. My mother worked to help support the family because most of my father's money was used for liquor. She did her best to shield me from his alcohol-induced rages. All in all, though, I thought I had a normal life. I played baseball, swam, rode bikes, and did all the other things children normally do. The biggest difference was that I spent as much time away from my family as I could to avoid the abuse at home.

When I was eleven, one of my cousins opened a whole new world to me—the world of masturbation. Little did I realize then that it would become my best friend, comforter, confidant, healer of hurts, medicine for my nerves, emotional support, and eventually my destroyer. I became a masturbation addict because it seemed to satisfy all my emotional needs. It was my secret. It never said no. It always had time for me and was always "there for me." It filled a hole in my soul that nothing and no one else could fill.

As I grew older, I became active in sports and community activities and did well in school. I had a normal high school life with many friends and girlfriends, but I was too shy to try to initiate sexual activity with the girls I went out with. My hormones were raging, but I managed to hide it, and I had a reputation as a nice guy. Little did these girls know that masturbation was my constant companion. Yet I longed for a girl who would let me satisfy my lusts. I thought that once I had a girl like that, I would be released from bondage; there would be no need to keep acting out. Was I wrong! After I found such a girl, the addiction prodded my mind to keep reliving our time together over and over. The mind is the strongest sex tool I possess. Now that I knew what sex was like, I could bring up a picture in my mind of any girl I wanted and fulfill my fantasies with her.

After graduation I went to college and found what I thought was a sexual utopia. The girls were much more available than high school girls. It seemed as if sex was there for the taking whenever I wanted, and I had an insatiable appetite. With all this sex, I expected my addictive behavior and emotional neediness would be cured, or at least diminished. Wrong! They just got stronger.

After college I got a good job with the government. I dated regularly and started feeling the need to find someone who could give me all the love, emotional support, and sexual fulfillment I longed for. I thought that once I found such a person, I could be free of the crippling emotional addiction that still had me turned upside down. I was acting out all the time and hated being a slave to it.

God led me to a woman who became my wife after a year of courtship. She was a virgin and let me know that she intended to stay that way until marriage. All I knew was that this lovely creature was all that I could ever ask for in a mate. She was loving, emotionally strong, organized, athletic, a nondrinker, nonsmoker, pretty, had a great figure, and was fun to be with. Why, Lord, did you send me such a wonderful woman who says no to premarital sex? This question would be answered almost thirty years later.

We married and had two wonderful children whom we loved and supported the best we could. I was determined that they would get all the emotional support that I never got while I was growing up. I had a faithful and responsive wife, yet I felt guilty because I was still deeply involved with my other loves—fantasy and masturbation. I kept this hidden from my wife and family.

On the outside, I was a moral person. I didn't have any girlie magazines around. I didn't rent pornographic movies. We were faithful in church, and I even held a responsible service position in that church. I prayed every day that God would remove this addictive burden from me. I found enough strength to avoid acting out with others, and the masturbation declined in frequency. I fooled myself into thinking that I was cured. The only problem remaining was some fantasies, and I discounted those. Appearances can be so deceiving! I deceived myself as well as the people around me.

I bought a computer when everyone else did. I needed one of those useful, innocent machines that help you become more organized. I needed to subscribe to a service which would open up the entire Internet universe and its unlimited information to me. Everything I ever wanted to know or see was now only a few keystrokes or clicks away. I could converse with people all over America and the world via email. Eureka! The third day I was online, I received an email with an attachment which simply said, "Hi, I just want to welcome you to the Internet. I am sending you my picture so you will know what I look like if you would like to talk with me sometime." People are so friendly on the Internet!

The note said, "Click here to see me." There have been thousands of times I have wished that I had never clicked that attachment, because it started a downward spiral that would lead to ruin. The woman, posed erotically, instructed me that if I wanted to see more of her and her girlfriends, I could join their club for a fee. A few minutes and a few keywords later, I was looking at more site descriptions than my monitor screen could hold. Click, click, click! To use an old Southern term, I was in "hog-heaven." So many pictures, so little time! My computer was in a back bedroom/den combination, and I could view it without being observed by my family. If I heard someone coming, I would quickly exit those sites and bring up wholesome sites on the screen.

It was only a few days before I was back into masturbation. I began to spend more and more time with the computer and less and less time with my family. It wasn't long before I was spending eight to twelve hours each day on the computer. I thought this was harmless. I began to visit illegal websites. That brought back all the wild fantasies I had had when I was growing up. I searched for more and more of these sites. I downloaded photos and traded with others online to get new and better ones.

This computer addiction continued for eight months. Then I received a call from a member of our church, who knew that I was a professional photographer, asking if I would take a few photos of his daughter which she could send to a modeling company for consideration. "Of course," I replied. She came to the photo session with several nice outfits. As the session went on, the subject of nude photography came up. My head buzzed with excitement. "Drop the subject now!" my sane mind told me—but my addicted, lustful mind was screaming, "Go for it!" Of course I listened to my sick mind, because I was living in the addiction. I took six nude photos of her, which I told myself were artful and not erotically posed. I told her that after she had seen the finished photos, we were going to destroy them and the negatives. I was afraid I would be in trouble if they were discovered.

The police were waiting for me the day I went to deliver the photos to her. I felt like I had been dropped into a bottomless pit. I dreaded having to make that phone call to my wife to let her know what I had done. My hidden secrets would now be on public display—and what a display! The television news and local newspaper had a field day with the story. While I was in jail awaiting a bond hearing, one of the other prisoners told me that I was getting more news coverage than he was, and he had killed someone! I was facing a ten-year sentence on a charge of sexual exploitation of a minor. While waiting to go to trial, I was fired from my civil service job of almost thirty-two years.

I voluntarily put myself into a treatment program. As part of the treatment, we attended SA meetings. I got a temporary sponsor, and I got sober. I knew I had a problem; now I had to deal with it. I phoned the SA Central Office and learned there was a group in my own city. When I got home, I went to a meeting and got a warm welcome. I found a sponsor and started working the Steps.

Back in court, I entered into a plea bargain on the advice of my attorney; I thought I could avoid prison time beyond the days I had spent in the county lock-up. My world collapsed again when I heard the judge sentence me to eighteen months in prison, to be followed by eight-and-a-half years on probation. The district attorney said I would only have to serve about six months in prison, because most prisoners serve about a third of their sentence. Wrong again! I wound up spending the entire eighteen months in prison. I was supposed to go to a minimum-security prison, but there was no space. I went to a maximum-security prison instead. My first and second cellmates were murderers serving life-without-parole sentences. Assaults, rapes, inhumane treatment—I saw it all during those eighteen months. I had to rely on my Higher Power to keep me safe. I read the Bible more in those eighteen months than I had in the previous fifty years.

I was able to attend open AA meetings, and thus continue working my Twelve Step program, by identifying as an adult child of an alcoholic. Through weekly correspondence, I was in touch with the other members of my home SA group; they encouraged me to work the Steps and stay sober. All the sick sexuality going on around me disgusted me to the point that I had little temptation to fantasy or masturbation.

On my release from prison, my family gave me a loving welcome home. My wife stuck with me, even though I had told her, at the time of my arrest and notoriety, that the best she could do for herself was to divorce me. I got back to my SA group immediately. I found a church that welcomed me and my family, and one of the men in the church got me a job in sales. The man who hired me knew about my record. He said it was not his duty to judge me, since the courts had already done that.

I have been sober since 1997. I work the Steps with my sponsor. He is the building guide who helps me lay a foundation for recovery, erect strong supports, build protective walls, set windows to see clearly through, and build a durable roof to help me weather the storms he knows I will go through. I don't always agree with what he tells me, but I try his suggestions. They have always worked for me, even when I said, "No way!" He has never let me just get by on a Step; he has to see that I understand it before we go on to the next one.

Service is part of my recovery. I now have the chance to carry the message to other suffering sexaholics. The SA Correctional Facilities Committee (SACFC) approached me about working with those who are headed for prison or who are in prison now. I see that my experience can benefit others as I correspond with prisoners and serve as a member of the SACFC. I also share the SA message with prison officials, who need to know the value of the SA program to those in their care. This has been my opportunity to really work the Twelfth Step.

I firmly believe that I had to go through my trials so that I could learn the power of surrender and then share my message with others. Surrender is essential to my daily recovery. I had to go through prison to learn my lesson, but my Higher Power knew what was best for me and I am truly grateful for the gift of surrender. Surrender is not easy for someone with a God-complex, because I have this need to feel in control.

As I write, my state's legislature is completing work on several bills that may affect me as a convicted sex offender. I don't know what those bills will look like when they become law, but some of the proposals reported in the news give me fear for myself and my family. My program tells me that God is in charge here, as in all things. I must ask God for the grace to surrender my will, let go of the fear, and live sober today.

4. Under New Management

One day while walking to elementary school, I made an important decision. I gave up trying to have friends. I determined to be satisfied with reading books and building models by myself. I felt as though I didn't belong anywhere or with anyone.

As a young boy, I was molested several times by older boys. I learned to masturbate from one of them. Sexual fantasies involving other boys came to me at odd times. I admired and sometimes worshipped older boys. I longed for their acceptance and approval.

I succeeded at sports and schoolwork, but felt I never measured up to anyone's expectations. Growing up, I went out with a few girls. I could only get close to them physically, never emotionally. I saw myself as a disappointment, especially to women. I felt I was a freak—abandoned, unloved, unlovable.

I was driven to find the magic pill that would make me normal. I tried golfing, hunting, fishing, track and field, working with machines, and even adopting what I thought were masculine mannerisms. I hoped just growing older would solve my problems. I read books that I hoped would lead me out of homosexuality, because I thought that was my problem. I tried various religious disciplines. Psychology seemed the next best solution. Over a period of thirteen years, I paid a psychologist and three counselors to help me.

I can't say I made a conscious decision, but I slowly drifted toward what was to become comfortable, the gay culture. I began to spend time at bars, restaurants, bath houses, beaches, and other places where gay men gathered. In a sexually-charged setting, I knew how to act. I felt alive, in control, and that others admired me. Lust allowed me to feel bigger, stronger, and better looking than I was accustomed to feeling.

At first, the anonymous sex was only occasional. Then it escalated. For the next ten years, I went out three or four times a week and usually had sex with multiple partners each time. Every now and then, I entertained hope that I was beginning a relationship with one of my sex partners. I was mistaken. He only wanted sex, and I only wanted sex with him. Neither of us was capable of giving more. Looking back, it seems we took turns using each other.

When I saw an attractive man, I nearly fell apart. I would do anything to unite myself with that person, to draw from him everything I thought I lacked. I wanted men to be fathers, teachers, guides, protectors, and providers for me. I was dependent and afraid of life. I desperately clung to the belief that if only a man would reach out to me, I would be changed forever. After sex, and sometimes before, my partner might say or do something that would destroy the illusion I had about him. That illusion grew from my belief that he was something more than human, or at least greater than I, and thus able to be for me all that I desired. Sometimes during sex with the "perfect partner," I sensed the reality that I could not extract from this experience what I really wanted. For years I lived an empty life, looking for someone else to fill it.

At age thirty-six I found Sexaholics Anonymous. I went to meetings for six years without getting sober. I had three sponsors during that time. What kept me coming for six years without success? SA members loved me enough to encourage me to keep coming back.

One night at a meeting, I saw a friend whom I hadn't seen in about a year. He had changed. He used to be scared and nervous. We used to talk on the phone about how we experienced lust, trying to find ways to live without it. Neither of us could. That night he was calm and self-assured. He asked if I wanted to be sober. I replied that I did.

He recruited a sponsor for me. My new sponsor told me to call him every day. I went home that night with no great expectations. I had no faith that I could ever be sober. However, I was willing to take the actions I was told to take. I had one phone number of a sex partner. I threw it away. Under the direction of my sponsor, I started to work the Steps as they are laid out in the book *Alcoholics Anonymous*.

The First Step says that I am powerless and my life is unmanageable. I stopped trying to change myself and my unmanageable feelings. One barrier to recovery was my fear of other men. I was always overcome with a dreadful feeling that I was doing something wrong or that I just wasn't enough. My old solution was to walk away. In recovery, I stay with the men God puts around me.

The Second Step, which says we came to believe that a Power greater than ourselves could restore us to sanity, meant more as I proceeded through the following Steps. Now I see that I had more faith in my feelings than in God. It was insane to believe in a solution rooted in lust. As I stay sober and work the Steps, my belief grows that God can deal with my problems.

In the Third Step, I asked God to relieve me of the bondage of self. I became willing to let God direct my life, showing me how to use it for the benefit of others. I let go of my own agenda for satisfying my needs and for achieving my plans for life in general. This surrender includes my sexual preference.

Today I am open to God. I accept what God gives. I now believe sex is optional; it is not essential in the experience of life. God's will is essential. Relationships based on love are essential. The experience of God's presence is essential for me to have a life worth living.

5. All in My Head

Sex was the dominant thing in my mind from my earliest memory. I was deeply obsessed about what was under my cousins' dresses from the time I was in first or second grade. Lots of kids tried to play doctor, but for me it was an intense preoccupation. When an older boy taught me to masturbate at eleven or twelve, I really got into that and into the fantasies I needed for my masturbation.

It soon got so the high point of each day would be when night came. I could get into bed, parade my sex fantasy through my head, and masturbate. I had slept in a bedroom with my younger brother. When the masturbation started, I moved into another bedroom to be free to masturbate. This left my younger brother deserted and alone.

Masturbation stepped up in frequency to three to five times a day. I kept trying to stop, but there was no stopping. I found a piece of pornography and hid it up in the haymow of our small barn in that little town. I would disappear from my friends and my brother and sneak off to the haymow to masturbate.

I didn't dare ask the girls in our small town for dates, so I asked girls from other towns instead. The minute I would catch someone, I lost interest in her and chased another one. I would often be chasing two or more at the same time.

This pattern continued through high school, the Air Force, into college, and up to the time I got married. I was very attentive to my wife during courtship. I wooed her with flowers, cultural events, plays, symphonies, and hockey and basketball games. The minute we got married, my attentions to her stopped. I switched addictions and became a workaholic. I lost myself in my work, hunting, and hobbies for twenty years. There were only brief times when my sexual addiction flared up.

After a heart attack, I changed careers and became a college teacher. Then I had another heart attack and faced heart surgery. Everything started to change. I lay in the hospital waiting to be strong enough for surgery. In my fear, I reached out to the young nurses for comfort, just as I had done five years earlier in the hospital after my first heart attack. There were long, intense discussions. Sometimes there would be three or four nurses in the room at one time. There would be wine parties late in the evening. The nursing supervisor became suspicious that something sexual was going on, but there wasn't, on the surface. I was outraged at her suspicions of me.

After surgery, things settled down for about two years before erupting again. I was putting out sexual innuendos, and my women students started coming to my office in response. I got more and more sexual with more and more students. A few months after that, I had surgery for what was thought to be cancer and was told that I would be dead in three weeks. The fear was overwhelming; my skin felt like it was burning with waves of fear. It turned out the doctors were wrong and the "inoperable" tumor went away. I came home and immediately sought my comfort in sexual contact with students. Sometimes I told myself that what I was doing wasn't wrong, because there was no intercourse, yet I would wake up in the middle of the night with a terrible fear. I prayed for the strength to stop, but I couldn't.

I got so out of control with my students that I found a way to resign my teaching job. In my business travels I got into a number of affairs. An intense affair, coupled with sex with other women at the same time, finally forced me to see how powerless and out of control I was. I gave up the affair, all sexual relationships, and gradually reduced the flirtations and coming-on to women I met. I still used the mental videotapes of those past experiences as tranquilizers to put me to sleep at night, or as comfort when I was troubled. I didn't see anything wrong with what I was doing, even though I had been in another Twelve Step program for seventeen years.

Finally, my wife got enough recovery to realize that she could not stand my behavior any more. She told me to get into SA or get out. I called the number she gave me. The man said, "It's lust, it's what's in your head that is killing you." That was the greatest relief in my life. In the other Twelve Step program, I had had a sponsor with many years experience, yet he and I couldn't figure out what was wrong. He used to tell me that people couldn't work that program if they were on another mood-altering chemical, like tranquilizers or marijuana. Here I was using what was for me the strongest drug, sexual excitement, and I didn't even know it. My lust had been my dependable friend for so long that I hadn't had the slightest suspicion it was really my problem.

Because I now had the Twelve Step program of Sexaholics Anonymous, I knew I never needed to lust again, with God's help, one moment at a time. I found that because of my sexual thinking, I had failed to be a husband to my wife, a father to my children, or a friend to my brother or to other men and women. I was so sick of what lusting had cost me that I immediately did everything I could think of. Every time lust came, I asked God to take it away. If it didn't go away, I would recite a prayer. I would keep reciting that prayer until the lust was gone. I gave my First Step to the group right away and felt an overwhelming relief. Immediately my wife saw a change in me. She said, "You aren't stiff and guarded anymore. You're finally the man I married, but couldn't find after our marriage." Just a month later, a son and a daughter who were counselors both said, "Dad, you're different."

My time in recovery has been spent going to meetings, working the Steps, reaching out to others, and practicing these principles in all my affairs. Close and loving relationships developed with men first, and much later with a few women. I'm gradually coming out of my isolation into intimacy. There is a growing love and emotional intimacy in our marriage. The years of abuse have severely impaired my sexual functioning, but that's all right. The growing strengths in other aspects of the marriage help make up for that.

I love this program. I put it ahead of everything else because it saved my life by helping guide me toward the real Connection. There is a deep love and closeness in our SA group and in the fellowship. Here I'm home.

6. A Legacy of Recovery

My first recollections of my addiction are from the summer my family moved to a new subdivision. I would be nine in August. The only other boy in the neighborhood was four years older, and he was lonely, since his parents both worked. We began to spend time together, and since he had a house all to himself, most of our time together was spent there. It was in the privacy of his house one day that he introduced me to pornography. The pictures hidden in his father's dresser drawer were tame by today's standards, but they were very compelling to me. My heart raced and I tingled with excitement. When he suggested that we remove our clothes and smoke cigarettes, the pictures took on a whole new dimension. I was hooked from the first viewing and craved opportunities to get lost in this exciting new experience.

The escape was a welcome relief from my family life. When I was five, my mother had given my father an ultimatum to quit drinking or risk losing his family. He had begun to slip into periods of deep depression during which he would retreat to his bedroom and not speak to the family for several days. When he did speak, he would rage at my mother and threaten to leave the family. I developed a sixth sense for gauging my father's moods the instant I walked into the house. I escaped from the tension and abuse at home by turning to the pleasure that the pictures provided. My friend soon explained how to masturbate to increase the sensations, and I would spend countless hours for the next twenty-four years trying to achieve the ultimate sensory experience. I knew instinctively that I needed to keep my discovery to myself, and I began to live in a secret world protected by lies and deceit. My life began to revolve around the adrenaline rush of finding a way to feed this insatiable hunger. I dreamed of possessing the objects of my lust, even though I wasn't quite sure what I would do with them if I had them.

Over the years I required ever more explicit pornography to maintain or increase the level of excitement. I connected with friends who had porno stashes of their own. We would go to R- and X-rated movies that offered the next plateau of excitement. My slow physical development and the shame I felt about my body prevented me from dating until college. The pent-up demand for physical contact with a woman was almost overwhelming. My first objective upon entering a relationship was to progress physically as quickly as possible. When I began having intercourse at age twenty-one, masturbation was still my constant companion. I used it as a panacea, a medicine to cure all my ills—when I was restless and wanted to sleep, when I was tired and wanted energy, when I was happy and deserved a treat, when I was sad and needed a lift.

As I got older, I decided that what I wanted in a relationship was the ultimate private stash. She needed to be intelligent and personable. More importantly, she had to have the right type of body and enjoy sex as much as I did. I married her when I was twenty-seven years old. I threw away my porno stash because I didn't think I needed it anymore. After all, we would have sex whenever I wanted it, wouldn't we? At first I masturbated only when she was having her period—because I needed the release, I told myself. As the frequency of sex in our marriage decreased, I began to fill in the dry periods with masturbation. I looked forward to my private time when I could engage in my addiction at my leisure, usually with the R-rated movies on cable TV.

My behavior started to change two years into our marriage, when I began my search for God. I became aware of how much time I was wasting with my sexual behavior. I tried to change: I had cable removed, I started to go to church again, and I tried to cut back on the masturbation, which I still kept secret from my wife. I had limited success. I could go dry for periods of time, but I would always fall back on my old behavior and feel completely defeated by it.

Four years into my marriage the pieces began to fall into place when by accident I turned on a TV talk show. I realize now that this coincidence was one of the many miracles that my God has worked in my life. The program dealt with sex addiction and featured a man sitting behind a screen describing his addictive behavior. He was telling *my* story! I felt sick; my worst fears were confirmed. I really was a low-life. I stopped masturbating immediately. I assumed that, like the alcoholic, I couldn't indulge in my drug any longer. What I didn't know was that I could not quit on my own, without support. The next year was a blur that culminated in separation from my wife and near loss of my job. During the stress of these events, I had returned to my drug. I was convinced that while I needed to stop, I could not.

Through another miracle of God, I learned about SA the following year, when I was thirty-two years old. That was 1985. I stopped masturbating, one day at a time, a week before my first meeting. I came to the meeting scared, alone, and embarrassed. I knew what it was that I needed and wanted to stop doing. I was completely in the dark about how to go about it. I shared my story and heard others share theirs. The relief was indescribable. But the temptation to masturbate did not disappear. I needed to work the Steps, to pray, and to use the telephone when the urge overcame me. As I withdrew from my addictive behaviors, I learned that *every aspect of my life was influenced by my addiction.* Slowly I began to replace the destructive behaviors with healthy ones, as I became aware of them. My sobriety in this program has allowed me to begin to feel my feelings instead of covering them with my drug.

I had been divorced for two years when I relocated to a new city because of my job. I had learned in my recovery to that point that my identity as a man needed to be affirmed by other men, not by the women whom my lust told me that I needed. I found our fellowship to be a safe haven where I could learn to become emotionally intimate with other recovering men. I learned valuable lessons about seeking friendships with people who wanted the same recovery I wanted and about letting go of acquaintances who were centered around how they looked on the outside. After some success with my male relationships, the fellowship provided an opportunity to become emotionally intimate with women, again in the safety of our fellowship bond.

After four and a half years of sobriety, I took the next step in my relationship recovery by asking a woman out on a date for dinner. During that first evening, as my mind contemplated spending a lifetime with this person, I could hear my sponsor's voice, also in my head, reminding me that this was about dinner! A lifetime relationship is built on the solid foundation of emotional intimacy, and that takes a lot of time and patience.

My dating experience ebbed and flowed over the next six years. Only after I had come to peace with living life as a single man, and with the idea of living the remainder of my life that way, did I meet the woman who was to become my wife. My newfound serenity gave me the freedom to risk letting her know who I really am. I shared about what I think and what I feel. My honesty was like a clear shining light to her. While my desire to refrain from any physical contact confused her at first, she felt encouraged enough to continue dating me. Once she learned about my recovery, many of her questions were answered. New ones replaced them, such as discussing the appropriate amount of physical contact for an engaged couple. With the support of my sponsor and others in the program who had preceded me in dating and marriage in sobriety, our courtship and engagement were a wonderful time of preparation for, and anticipation of, our new life together. As my wife, she continues to support my recovery. Words cannot express the joy that she has brought into my life.

Our marriage has been unbelievably blessed by God. When I shared the good news of our pregnancy with my sister, and the discovery that we were going to have a son, her response was that the cycle was coming full circle. I was being given a chance by God to pass on a new legacy of sobriety and recovery to my son, one that he could pass on to his children.

I am a recovering sexaholic, and I am reminded daily that I will be a sexaholic for the rest of my life. My addiction is never far from me. It may appear in the form of the sudden recollection of some past sexual encounter. I have the option of calling upon my God to take this uncomfortable memory away. I can connect instead with Him, the Source of my strength. I am reminded nearly every time I attend a meeting where I could be today if God had not made Himself known to me. Through the fellowship of this program, I am learning to relate to others and to let go of all the defenses that served me so well in my childhood, but which were so destructive in my adult life. I am so grateful to my brothers and sisters in this program who have shared their lives with me so that I could be freed from this terrible bondage. I am deeply humbled by the grace of God that I have found in this fellowship, and I plan to keep coming back, one day at a time.

7. Getting Real

All I ever wanted was someone to love me. This is a natural instinct, but I didn't know that I would seek out unnatural ways to fill the hole in my soul. I grew up the eldest of three girls in a suburban home. My parents had their own issues to battle. My father was an alcoholic and a sexaholic, and my mother enabled him. My father indulged in soft porn. There was some talk of body parts. He had an affair with a show girl on a business trip, an abortion was involved, and nobody talked about it. He drank over this woman and played gypsy violin music late and loud.

I medicated by touching myself, being naked outdoors, or showing myself while playing doctor with a couple of the neighbor children. I didn't feel loved, but I was okay with life until I started school. I didn't know how to operate in classroom groups or how to make friends. It seemed like the other kids were smarter, and I was just guessing at what to do. I felt I was different, I wasn't enough, I was ignored. There was something wrong with me.

When I got to college, I began to have sex with others. At that time, I believed that it was the only way I could feel close or make any kind of connection with other people, although—funny thing—my "relationships" never went anywhere. My acting out soon progressed to promiscuity. I flunked out of college, moved to another city, started attending an art school, lived with a sexaholic drug dealer I'd met at a bus depot, went to jail for a weekend, engaged in public sex and sex with multiple partners. I was miserable.

As my disease continued to drive me, I acted out in anonymous sex. I found the anticipation and the game exciting. I was the spider luring the fly into her web! I was getting sicker and sicker, and I was sick of being me. My life was unmanageable, as I moved between the city and home seven times in four years. I was an emotional mess. I gave up, returned home, and a week later my dad died.

I thought bars would be a good place to take care of my feelings and socialize with others, but after nine months of going home with strange men, I had had enough. Then my 23-year-old sister committed suicide.

I decided to go "wholesome." I baked whole grain bread, made quilts and soap. I joined a church. I quit smoking, getting drunk, and chasing men. I married and had two children. Surely all these changes would turn my life around. My past was wrapped and tied and stashed away under the extra blankets in the closet. I'd be okay now. I was faithful to my husband for sixteen years, but I was still very unhappy because I felt we were not an appropriate match. When my church's doctrines on divorce and remarriage changed, I joined the ranks of single parents. For a couple of years I was okay. I didn't need men.

I resisted the desire to masturbate on religious grounds. Then a therapist challenged me on my religious beliefs. I called church headquarters to check and learned that masturbation was considered a "natural" outlet. I began masturbating compulsively. The past that I thought was tightly secured jumped out of the closet and unwrapped itself. I got on-line and immediately became addicted to chat rooms. I'd stay up all night three times a week on the computer and then go to work, robbing my employer of my full presence at work. I wrote erotic fantasies to strange men, had phone sex while my children were in the house. I felt dual: the woman who led the church children's choir and believed that sex was only for marriage, and the woman who engaged in emotional prostitution on-line. It was like two separate movies were running inside me at the same time. I met a decent man at church who wanted my companionship only, so I had to seek out the sex I wanted elsewhere. Finally, I started meeting in person with men that I'd chatted with on-line.

I was always in fantasy. I made a tape of romantic musical accompaniment for my time in the car, sugary melodies oozing out the "movie" of me—charming, irresistibly seductive, long-legged, and beautiful. I drove with the sun roof open, ogling men in traffic, imagining what we would say and do together, flirting in a sparkling, rarified atmosphere. Preoccupied with these fantasies while driving in the city, I'd end up on the other side of town without knowing how I got there.

I became concerned that the space between my sexual acting out episodes grew shorter and shorter and confided in a new man at church. As Providence would have it, he was in SA and invited me to a meeting. When I went there, I entered a room of mostly men. Attending was not always pleasant or easy, and I must admit I didn't take the whole thing seriously. I knew I had a problem, but I just couldn't say I was a sex addict. All I could say with any certainty was that I was out of reality. My life was indeed unmanageable.

I got a sponsor and did what she told me. She told me to attend and share in at least three meetings a week. Usually I went to six. Because my sponsor told me not to call men the first year, I became careful with my eyes. I became quite an expert on men's shoe styles. My sponsor told me I was a predator so I grew careful about whom I spent time with and around. No more lingering near men in the grocery store aisles. She told me I was romantically enmeshed with my male friend; I said an extremely difficult goodbye. My sponsor helped me through an unexpected attraction to a female sponsee. I came to understand that I was trying to run my own show, trying to be my own Higher Power. I really *did* have a problem!

I thought that I was hard boiled, that the Steps wouldn't work for me—but I worked Steps One to Nine in the first year and a half. With Step One I began to feel *a part of* instead of *apart from*. I felt a great peace after completing Step Five. But my favorite Steps were Eight and One-Half, forgiveness as explained in *Sexaholics Anonymous* (125-26), and Nine, as illustrated in the AA Big Book (552). I prayed through the list of persons I resented, morning and night, wrote my letters to each person, and made my amends to everyone, including my children. I went to retreats and did service there. I served as intergroup secretary and chairperson. I became a reader for SA publications. After several false starts and demoralizing failures, I was given sobriety in 2000 and am now in my sixth year.

Recovery has given me the freedom to address outside issues. I discovered I had attention deficit hyperactive disorder (ADHD) and other mental health issues and began taking medication; people tell me that I appear more relaxed and stable.

I feel safe, accepted, respected, and supported in recovery. My relationships with both men and women have deepened. Most important, I have the hope of a loving and helping relationship with God. I'm coming into reality. I don't always like it, I'm often afraid, but I have a better chance to live a good life this way than the way I was before. My path opens ever wider before me.

8. It Has to Be a Miracle!

I was forty-four years old, had been married for twenty-three years, was the father of four children, and had a successful career. Yet I was leaving a porno store, disgusted with myself once again. It was hopeless. Anonymous sex had become a daily occurrence. I knew I was going to lose my wife, my children, and my profession. I was ready to lose it all rather than fight the compulsion one more moment.

Within one hour from that moment of utter defeat and despair, I met the man who had previously informed me about Sexaholics Anonymous. I told him I was ready. He handed me the SA brochure. I read it and told myself there was a mistake in this brochure. To me it said, no sex with self. As a man of science, I knew that could not be accurate: masturbation was normal! Then, deep within me, I finally understood. This was my drug. I had previously tried not having sex outside my marriage, but the true culprit turned out to be masturbation. Everything built on top of that realization. It was a moment of clarity. It was a miracle.

By age five I was already masturbating and being sexual with a neighborhood girl. By age ten I began fantasizing about my Sunday school teacher and his wife. I would picture them engaged in sex together. At that same age I can remember being mesmerized by naked men in a locker room at a day camp I was attending.

When I was eleven, my parents decided to move to another state. There, I went to school in a neighborhood that was quite hostile to people of my religion. Some older boys befriended me and offered me protection, but in return I had to be sexual with them. This lasted for about three months. It led me to believe that male friendship must include sexual contact.

During my teenage years, I became obsessed with being as sexual as I could with the girls I dated. There was also some sexual experimentation with boys my age, especially with those who befriended me. From age fourteen to age seventeen there was an incestuous relationship with my male cousin. When I turned sixteen, my uncle decided I should be initiated into manhood by visiting a prostitute. It was a dismal failure sexually for me, and a deathblow to my emerging sense of self. I spent the rest of my high school years trying to prove I was sexually adequate with women. The result was sexual obsession and abuse of all the girls I dated.

In college I met my future wife. From the onset, I became sexually obsessive and abusive with her. Masturbation in secret continued. I was twenty-one when we married. I continued to have frequent sex with her to the point where she took me to her gynecologist. He told me I was acting like a "sex maniac." I thought both of them were crazy. I was able to stop masturbating for the first few weeks of our marriage, but soon the secret behavior started again. For the first twelve years of our marriage there were only rare indiscretions, but in fantasy I was unfaithful many times. Then one day at a local health club I discovered promiscuous sex with men. I was like a duck in water.

For the next ten years my sexual behavior was out of control. I was having sex with hundreds of partners, buying sex from men and women, and practicing group sex, exhibitionism, and voyeurism. I would spend money on my sex partners instead of spending it on my family. I could not pay for my children's college tuition. I would develop obsessions toward these partners, becoming possessive, jealous, and full of rage. I put my family and myself in dangerous situations. I brought diseases home to my wife. Time and again I would cry to my wife, "Never Again!"—only to succumb within hours. I would make oaths to God to stop, but soon I would be acting out again.

My addiction took me to the gates of hell, but I could not turn back. Seven months prior to attending my first SA meeting, I discovered the wonder of Twelve Step recovery through Alcoholics Anonymous. I would leave the AA meeting and jog down to a porno shop for anonymous sex. I stopped drinking, but would not stop acting out—yet I knew that my acting out would lead to a relapse in AA. I could not do Steps Six and Seven because I was not entirely ready to have God remove all my defects of character. I did not want to stop acting out sexually, and I knew that without completing my Step work I could not stay sober from alcohol. It was on that day, after leaving the porno shop in utter hopelessness, that I met the person who had previously informed me about SA. He invited me to my first SA meeting. I was ready. It was just the two of us at that first meeting. What has happened since that day is the miracle of sobriety.

Stopping the use of my drug was a day-by-day drudgery. We had only one SA meeting a week back then. That one night a week was sacred to me. One day at a time, I learned about sobriety. The SA manual had not been published yet, but we had that cherished SA brochure with "The Solution" that said it all for us. People came to the meetings. People stopped coming to the meetings. Even the person who founded SA in our community stopped attending. That first year I counted 120 people who came and went. There were two people left at the end of that year, and thank God I was one of them. Since then, I have watched our fellowship grow to many meetings a week with many members having long term sobriety.

How did I stay sober back then with no SA book and only one meeting a week? One day at a time, that's how! I would make a contract each day with God. I would promise just for that day that I would stay sexually sober. I told God that I could not guarantee tomorrow. I would then ask God to keep me sober for the next twenty-four hours. I learned how to avoid triggers, even those concerning my own body. I learned to pray for those people who were triggers to me. I got better.

Something was still missing. After eleven months of sobriety I began suspecting what it was. *Lust was still there being camouflaged as sex in marriage.* I realized I needed a period of sexual abstinence from my spouse. I fought the idea, but finally I asked my wife. She agreed. After six weeks of abstinence I told her I was ready to resume our sexual relationship. With hatred in her eyes and voice she said, "I'm not!"

Why was this a shock to me? This was the person I had sexually abused for twenty-four years. My sponsor said, "You're an addict. You cannot be the one to know when to stop your abstinence. Let

God talk through your wife." God did, almost two years later. For me it took twenty-one months of total sexual abstinence for that part of my illness to subside.

I received great gifts in this program. Once I let go of the masturbation, the sexual fantasies left. I still occasionally have what I call two-dimensional sexual photographs in my head, but with prayer they leave quickly without developing into fantasies. I have also had the gift given to me of losing the desire to act out with people outside my marriage. Noticing body parts and experiencing erotic dreams took many years to subside.

My sexaholic mentality still flares up periodically. I will notice people in the street walking together and automatically wonder if they are lovers. I will observe people looking at me and for a moment think they are trying to seduce me. These thoughts happen less frequently now. When they do occur I pray, "God, whatever it is I am looking for in that person, may I find it in You." I thank God when these thoughts appear for reminding me I am still sick. How dangerous it would be to think I am cured!

There are character defects that are slow in leaving: greed, envy, and control, to mention only a few. The miracle is that they are lessening, and that I am aware of them when they appear. My sponsor told me that I am better than I used to be but not as well as I am going to get. I have learned new tools through the program to deal with my defects. Step Ten always works when I use it. To promptly admit my faults to myself and to another human being brings me immediate relief. A burden shared is half as heavy.

Other miracles have happened. I no longer have a preoccupation about my gender orientation. It was not an issue of "gay, straight, or bisexual." It was an issue of addiction. Once I put my drug away, those issues seemed to vanish, one day at a time.

Miracles are happening in our family. My spouse and I are more comfortable with each other than we have ever been. We try not to work each other's programs. We travel all over the world together, enjoying each other's company. We look forward to these times together. My children and I are getting along so much better.

When they were younger they would joke with us, saying, "Are you going to one of those 'Lust Buster' conferences again?" Now my children are older and three of them are married. My daughters-in-law know that I am in the program. They have an open invitation to ask me about my program, and I have the freedom if asked to tell them the simple truth. They trust me with my grandchildren. I feel the genuine love among us all.

Last but not least is the miracle of finding the God of my understanding, a God who watched me that day in the porno store and still loved me so much that He brought me to this wonderful fellowship of Sexaholics Anonymous. My God is my good friend today. I can talk to Him any time or place. I occasionally lapse back into the belief in a God of retribution, who is out to get me. When that happens I ask God to remove that thought from me. I know how much God loves me.

This is how I stay sober today. It is simple. I do the same things today I did when I first came into the program. I get on my knees each morning and evening to give my Higher Power my day. I pray for His will for me. I speak on the phone with people from the fellowship throughout the day and evening. I do a great deal of sponsorship; whatever the results for the sponsee, it helps me. I make a two-way contract with God each day. I ask God to keep me sober that day and tell God I will stay sober that day. I make a gratitude list each day to keep me currently connected to God. I try to attend a recovery meeting each day. I read from the SA manual or the AA Big Book.

My recovery is like a three-legged stool. The stool is sturdy and safe on its three legs. If any one leg breaks, the stool will topple. The three legs represent:

> The Twelve Steps of the program,
> The God of my understanding, and
> The fellowship of SA, both meetings and sponsorship.

If I use all three legs simultaneously, I am on solid ground. When I omit any one of the three, my program is in an unsafe condition.

I have been sober, one day at a time, since 1984. One day at a time, I want to stay sober. How else can I get to keep all I have found in this fellowship? I have found recovery in SA. I have found friendship. I have found a loving God. I have truly found my home. Each morning I make a decision to accept the gift of sobriety, and each day I receive it again. It has to be a miracle!

9. A Lady Can't Be a Sex Addict!

I was a lady, and a lady just can't be a sex addict! So I told myself when I thought of joining SA. No, I didn't have that problem—it was my ex-boyfriend's problem! The sexual practices that we argued about were not the problem. He just needed to stop taking care of his ex-wife.

Once in recovery I began to learn that my acting out was a perverted attempt to be appreciated, valued, loved. I didn't believe I was lovable, so instead I sought to be lusted after. I also learned that I acted out to feel powerful and to revenge myself against my ex-husband.

The core of my sexual addiction is relationship addiction. I learned about SA at the first Twelve Step meeting I attended (Adult Children of Alcoholics, or ACA). I went to SA the next week looking for help—for my ex-boyfriend! I could not see my own problem until one and one-half years later when I returned for myself.

Growing up in an alcoholic home meant that I often had to take on adult responsibilities for myself or my younger brothers. My parents were embroiled in their own struggles. I felt very alone. Dad was not only angry, short-tempered, and unable to keep a job; he threatened me if I didn't go to the local grocery store and buy his supply of beer. I felt as though everyone I met in the store and on the way home knew that I had a drunk for a father. At school I believed I was the only poor kid. I felt so much shame.

By the time I was fourteen, I went to one of the priests in my church and said I wanted help in believing in God. He spent a year trying to help me. When I went to college, I made sure it was a religious one so I could learn the answers to my need for God. I had no idea what it was about or why I so desperately needed to know or feel God's presence. I was sure everyone else believed and that they were secure and comforted in their faith.

The summer before my senior year I met the man I would marry. On our first date, we both declared our disgust with our parents' marital relationships and admitted we had no idea how to have a fulfilling marriage. A year and a half later we began duplicating their relationships in our marriage.

After seven years of marriage, I saw my husband touch a woman in our therapy group with tender affection. He told me he could only touch me in a sexual way. Within a week I acted out with another man. I went home and told my husband. I wanted him to be upset, jealous, *something!* He just said, "I guess we have an open marriage."

Before long, I had seduced someone else. I didn't know how or why, and it didn't make me feel any better. Instead, I felt confused and dirty and ashamed—that old familiar feeling. After that the men who were our friends seemed to know I was available sexually. My denial was so cunning that I couldn't understand how they knew, and I couldn't say no.

Two years later, I was divorced. Determined to overcome my prudishness, I spent a few years acting out and feeling worse. I remarked to a girlfriend that I wanted to stop having sex with men that I'd just met. She told me that I would stop when I got sick of it. I was sick of it, but I still could not stop. I didn't know then that I was addicted and that I had been addicted since the first time.

When I first attended ACA meetings, I knew that I had a problem getting too involved too quickly with men. I lost my identity and my life when I was in a relationship. After a while I decided that the way to avoid getting hooked by one man was to date several simultaneously. Another time I decided the problem was that I just couldn't go a year without dating. If I could just do that, I'd be okay and could marry again. Besides, the men who were interested in marrying me had problems I could not accept; I kept finding myself with addicts!

I continued in ACA and a women's therapy group. Twice I lost months of sobriety. Then I acted out with a man I met at a business meeting. I couldn't lie to myself any more. My therapist said it was SA or inpatient treatment for me.

That's when I started going to SA meetings for myself. During my first year or two, an ex-partner attended meetings as well; because I felt so unsafe with this man who had no sobriety, my sponsor allowed me to invite several other members to hear my First Step before the meeting. Afterward, she commented that she did not hear a lot about powerlessness and unmanageability, only about my being the victim.

Doing a Fourth Step in another program helped release me from the illusion of being a victim. When I did my Fourth in SA, I could be more forthright. After my Fifth Step, it was wonderful to "burn the evidence" against me and begin the road to forgiving myself. Therapy had given me awareness of how I was hurting others and myself, but it could not make me stop. After fifteen years of insanity, I was free now in SA.

Old boyfriends would call during that first year and even later, and I could say, "No, thank you." I even went to dinner with one, and God did for me what I was never able to do for myself. I called my sponsor after the fact. Was I lucky that time!

God granted my prayer to get out of sales jobs that were really a big source of triggers and partners. I started at a greatly reduced salary in a whole new area. Eventually I was able to return to school and complete a master's degree while on this job.

Four years into sobriety, my self-reliance was strong and my God-reliance was tenuous. I thought I knew everything. I had five sponsees and had done service work on the group, intergroup, and regional levels. I spent a lot of time helping others and not enough time keeping my house in order with prayer, meditation, journaling, and calls to my sponsor. I had problems with control, but I didn't see that because I didn't want to see it. I relapsed.

I made a date with a man to have dinner at a restaurant. Then I called my sponsor to work out how to protect my sobriety. What I didn't tell her was that I got high earlier that day merely holding his hand. I was drunk on lust. When he took me home, I engaged in physical foreplay with him. I gave away sex and my self-esteem, as I had done so many times in the past. I got nothing but physical pain and this devastating fear that I had made an unthinkable mistake.

I couldn't decide whether I had lost my sobriety. When my sponsor told me that I had, I was furious! How could she tell me that while I was at work? I shut the door to my office and cried uncontrollably for two hours. As reality sank in, I knew I had lied to myself and couldn't trust my own thinking. I had to let go of my pride and get back to work on my program.

It was two weeks before an SA international convention, and I had a plane ticket. I decided to go and give my First Step there. What I gained from giving my shame away so quickly was the most beautiful First Step imaginable. As God would have it, the room was packed with twenty to twenty-five people. There were unfamiliar faces, but there were also about a dozen folks from my town. Never have I felt closer to that bunch than after receiving their feedback and hugs that night.

The next day someone who did not come to my First Step remarked that I looked so much better than the day before. Wow—people could actually see a physical difference from my working a Step! I date my sobriety from that time in 1992.

My program has benefited from the relapse. I take joy connecting by telephone with other women. I attend meetings in my area, as well as those at the regional and international levels. I'm doing service work at the various levels, but my attitude is different. I set boundaries for my own good, for example, limiting myself to one service position at a time. I do the best I can at a task, and then I let it go. I'm not in control.

Today I have surrendered the right to seek a relationship with a man. If that would be good for me, then the God of my understanding will provide it. I am simply to thank my God for every experience and look for the lesson.

I did not return to my religion of origin, but I have found other spiritual resources. My old script was to remain poor of spirit and material gifts, but today my spirituality includes a belief in abundance. My life has changed as I change my thinking from self-defeating or fearful thoughts to gratitude and to affirmation of what I want in life. I have a fear of physical pain and incapacity because I have experienced these in the past; when those fears come to me, I say an affirming "Thank you for my good health!" I have a fear of not being able to meet my financial needs, and I'm afraid to spend money on myself; I affirm that all my needs are met and that I am worthy of having nice things. Now I notice and feel gratitude when material things come to me: I've been given free trips, a new car, a much nicer home, help in moving and repairing, a fulfilling career, help after three major surgeries, and other gifts too numerous to mention. I affirm that I deserve an abundant life. The intangible gifts are a warm relationship with my only child, gratitude and serenity instead of self-pity and fear, and the ability to allow others to say no. I can appreciate and learn from others rather than needing to teach them and have them appreciate me, and I can give without always expecting something in return.

I used to think that one of the benefits of my addiction was excitement. I was so afraid of being bored! Now my life is quieter. No adventure is worth sacrificing my peace of mind. Peace of mind is the only goal I ever want to seek.

10. I Can Never Take Recovery for Granted

When I was a boy growing up on a farm, I was very shy. It was hard for me to talk to anyone about sex. So when a neighbor boy introduced me to masturbation, I was ashamed to talk to anyone except the priest in the confessional. I knew there was something wrong about it, and I tried to stop many times. However, I was hooked on it. Without knowing it at the time, I was looking for the Big Fix. It was always, "Just once more before next Saturday's confession." Then I would think, "You've done it once, so why not do it again before you go to confession?" So I got in as much lust as I could before I went. After each confession, I would promise God that I would never do it again.

I felt that I was the most sexual person alive! I had sex on my mind all the time. Sexual arousal came at the most embarrassing times. It was never a question of *whether* to masturbate. Once aroused, I always ended up masturbating. I struggled with masturbation throughout my teens and into my early twenties. Then, for a time, I thought I had it under control.

Until that point, I had had no sex with others. In my late twenties, an older man invited me to a motel to "talk." I was an easy target, because I was passive and had no willpower to say no to sex. That night, I learned ways of acting out that I had never experienced. This opened up a whole new realm of lust. I became the pursuer. I pursued other men. I started cruising. I frequented bars looking for sex. There was never enough. My addiction had truly progressed during my twenties, even while I thought I was gaining some control over it.

When I couldn't find men, I pursued boys. I drank alcohol to numb feelings of guilt, inadequacy, shame, and emptiness. I would befriend a young person, telling myself I didn't intend to act out with him—but within a very short time I would be in bed with him. Afterward I would say, "This was the first time this ever happened and it will never happen again." The Big Lie. I would drop that partner and pursue the next one.

41

At the time, I was totally unaware of what I was doing to my victims. I was focused on my lust, unaware that I was trying to fill the emptiness within my soul with a distorted intimacy with another. My addictive behavior never met my need, that of making a real connection with God and other human beings. I felt alone. I could never reach out to anyone else—my life had become too shameful. I was living a Jekyll-and-Hyde existence. My addiction was controlling my life, and I saw no way out.

At the age of forty-six I finally sought help and was sent to a treatment center for sex addiction. I was so grateful for my introduction to Sexaholics Anonymous there. I embraced this program of recovery and began to work the Steps. For the first time in my adult life I felt that there was hope for me. It felt so good to be free of the power of the addiction. I was fortunate to be released from the obsession with sex from the beginning. I had an occasional fleeting thought or memory, but only infrequent sexual feelings or arousal. I traveled sixty miles to attend a weekly SA meeting because I knew my life depended on it. My whole week revolved around that meeting. I became active in SA and tried to put all the principles of the program into practice in my life. I was very disciplined and avoided any situations that would trigger me. I avoided getting into any male relationships, even appropriate ones, because I was afraid of what I might do. I wanted sobriety so badly!

For the first time in my life I began to feel alive. I began to experience feelings that I had never felt before. Life was not easy, but it was a hundred times better than when I was acting out. Each year of recovery, new discoveries unfolded. I was able to think more clearly. I was able to go for longer periods of time without being physically sick. I became calmer about events in my life, not letting people or situations get me upset. The more sobriety I attained, the more serenity came.

At eight years of sobriety, I attended an SA international convention and felt very pleased to go up in front of everyone and get my sobriety chip at the Friday evening birthday party. Then, within a week, I relapsed by masturbating.

This compulsion is very baffling and cunning, as well as powerful. I picture this disease as a large black panther waiting to pounce on me. It seems to know my weaknesses and my strengths and will attack me when I least expect it. I was alone and away from home, inside my secret self. My addiction tempted me: "Just this little bit of pleasure won't lead to masturbation. Go ahead and cross that boundary. It won't happen!" The Big Lie! By taking the first little step toward lust, I was lost. Since my slip I try not to over-analyze what happened, because one of my character defects is to judge and condemn myself. But there were signs along the way that I was heading for a fall. I had begun to take my sobriety for granted. I had begun to relax my reliance on the power of my God and to rely more on myself. I had begun to think that I had this addiction licked and—the ultimate temptation—that I was no longer a sex addict. I had slowed down on my Step work and had begun to cross the boundary from trusted servant to one who thinks he is better than others and knows more than others in the group.

Six months later, I went to the birthday party at an international convention with five months of sobriety and admitted that I had relapsed. I was filled with gratitude to have another chance to get sober. I know many who have gone back out and not returned. I can never take recovery for granted. I have been sober now since 1995, but I need to be wary of counting months or years of sobriety as something to be proud of. What's important is that I'm sober today.

11. A Change for the Better

I was a quiet, shy boy with very few friends. I felt that I was not as good as the other kids because I had no father and we were very poor. We were on welfare.

I believe I was a sexaholic at ten years old. I remember at that age undressing the girls in my classroom with my eyes. In my mind the girls were nothing more than robots. I was thirteen years old when I masturbated for the first time while fantasizing about girls. I thought that was the greatest pleasure I could ever feel, and I did it again and again as often as possible.

In my early teens I put on my mother's or sister's clothes a few times. I felt as if I was hurting them or getting even with them. When I took off their clothes I soiled them and destroyed them. The desire to put on their clothes drove me crazy, but when I did it I felt like a fool and took them off immediately.

I did not go out on dates with girls in my teens. That contributed to my feelings of being less adequate than other boys. All I did was fantasize and masturbate. To this day I have never had sex with anyone except myself.

When I was twenty years old, I started going to porno movies. When the other men at work talked about sex with their girl-friends, I was able to be part of the conversation by talking about what I had seen in porno movies. I usually stayed in the porno movie about thirty minutes. I would become angry and leave be-cause I knew that real women are not like that. I did not approve of the men who acted in the porno movie. They were doing what I wanted to do with women. Since I thought of myself as dirt, I con-sidered the men in the porno movies as dirt also. I felt angry about the movie, but a week or two later I would go back to see another one. I did not realize that I was addicted.

At this point I started buying cheap porno newspapers. I would buy one, take it home, look through the pages, masturbate, rip up the paper, and throw it away. A few days later I would buy another porno paper. I did this for about two months, never understanding why I was buying a paper only to rip it up and throw it away.

Eventually I found a paper that aroused my interest. It was about transvestites. I decided, "This is what I want to do." I bought women's clothing and other items I felt I needed to make the fantasy real. I waited until my family went away on vacation. I told them that I had to work and could not join them. When they were gone from the house, I took out the women's clothes from the closet. Pulling some items out of the bag, I looked at them, called myself an idiot, and threw it all away. The very next day I wished I still had the women's clothes. I did not understand—why did I still want them?

Finally, I found SA. When I went to my first meeting, I heard a piece of myself in the other people who shared. I could hardly believe that there were other people who thought like I did.

The next year I gave my First Step inventory. After I presented it, people came up to me to share ways they could relate to my story. I did not get a sponsor, and I rarely called anyone. I felt that I did not fully belong and did not join in any fellowship after meetings. I did not become sober. I continued to fantasize and masturbate daily. While I preferred to fantasize about women, I also fantasized about men, children, and animals.

The change came over a long holiday weekend in 1991. I was at a meeting, and someone asked me how I was doing. Usually I would answer that everything was okay, but this time I said I wasn't doing so well. I told him a little bit about my problems. For me, that was my real First Step. I got sober that weekend. In the beginning I was only physically sober. I was not fantasizing or masturbating.

After a few weeks of sobriety, I wondered why I was not acting out. I still wanted to act out, but I was not doing it. My conclusion was that my Higher Power was stopping me, and that I was listening to my Higher Power. That was my Second Step. When I saw an attractive woman, my head would immediately turn in the opposite direction. I came to believe that my Higher Power was turning my head away, because I still wanted to look. At that point I adopted the phrase, "Higher Power is keeping me sexually sober."

I was sober about two months when I became very angry. I argued that I just wanted to look at the women, nothing else. I started pounding my fist against my knee saying, "Why can't I just look?" Inside me I heard God's voice, and that voice said, "You just can't." I accepted that answer and remained sober. That was my Third Step.

I was sober about one year before I summoned enough nerve to ask someone to be my sponsor. He was really busy but he accepted me as a sponsee because he realized that it took a lot of effort on my part to ask. I called him on the phone about once a month. He never asked me to do anything, like actively work the Steps.

I was sober about two and a half years when someone offered to find a Step sponsor for me. My new sponsor was like a drill sergeant. He pushed me to work the Steps. He gave me one week to do my Fourth Step. It took me two weeks to do it, and then I gave him my Fifth Step. He asked me to make three program phone calls a day, which I did. I experienced a great deal of growth with that sponsor.

At a meeting when I shared, no one could question me. No crosstalk! When I called people on the phone, they would ask me questions. When they questioned me, it forced me to think. I started to understand what was wrong with me.

As I started to understand myself, I started to become emotionally sober. At that point I started to work the Steps in my daily routine in order to cope with all the little problems that occur in my life. In the past, I had hardly ever talked to my cousins, because I felt ashamed of my life. Making program phone calls made it easier to call my cousins. When I wasn't sober, I ran away or avoided problems and responsibility. As I started to grow, I grudgingly accepted my shortcomings and started to deal with them more positively.

I became involved with my intergroup and would accept responsibilities, such as planning a holiday party or a one-day conference. When I needed other members to help with preparations, I wanted them to help me immediately. It took a lot of crying to my sponsor before I began to accept that the help would come, but not necessarily at the moment I wanted it.

My experience doing service in SA has given me confidence to volunteer at work when we have our annual holiday party. Where I attend religious services, I help out by handing out books and preparing meals for some of the ceremonies.

One of the nicest gifts of the program is that I can finally accept a compliment. In the past if someone in my neighborhood remarked that I was a nice man and would make a good husband, I would wonder how she could possibly see anything good in me. I would become angry and depressed about what she had said to me. I could only see all the little things I do wrong.

I can see change in myself in the experience I had with a date. Afterward, it was clear that this woman was not interested in seeing me again. When I told my sister that she was not interested in me, she answered, "She's passing up someone good." I accepted what she said as a compliment. I have changed for the better.

12. A New Purpose in Life

I was forty-one years old and a graduate student in seminary. It was nearing midnight when I awoke with my heart pounding and my mind racing as I contemplated a new fantasy about how I could mix sexual pleasure with pain. My wife was asleep next to me, five months pregnant with our second child. Our three-year-old daughter was in her own room. I remembered that I had once told myself I would never act out around my family, but I'd crossed that boundary so often that my guilt for crossing it again was only fleeting. I would die if I didn't get the escape that came from acting out, yet I would die if I allowed it to go on much longer. I wanted to stop these behaviors, but at the same time I loved them more than life itself. I was willing to sell my soul in exchange for what they gave me.

That night, as I acted out while the family slept, I conceived of one last orgy of pleasure and pain that would end my life. In my fantasies, I was plunging toward death—and soon! I could not envision still being alive when my wife gave birth to our second child.

I didn't arrive at this depth of despair overnight. I'd been acting out for twenty-eight years. It began when I discovered at age thirteen that inflicting pain on myself gave me sexual pleasure. From then on, I was always looking for new ways to hurt myself; variety helped generate the adrenaline rush I needed. But the things I did made me feel isolated and different from other people. Slowly but surely my compulsion tightened its grip on my life, pulling me downward into uncharted depths. Each incident, each boundary violated, each individual harmed added to the weight of guilt, shame, and remorse.

Sex with self or another person became my main mechanism for coping with life. When I was stressed about something, I masturbated to relieve the pressure. When I was angry, I acted out to numb my feelings. When I was lonely, depressed, or afraid, I acted out to comfort myself. I had no choice.

After acting out, I felt utterly alone, alienated from God, from others, and from myself. I promised that I would never do it again. I tried to cover up all the evidence. I was plagued by feelings of guilt, remorse, and humiliation for what I had done. There was a growing split in my personality between who I was in the presence of those I loved and esteemed and who I was when I was alone, caught in the vise-like grip of this compulsion.

By the time I graduated from college, I'd begun to create opportunities to have unprotected sex with women. I was always seeking opportunities to look beneath the clothing of some unsuspecting female. I discovered that I was attracted to younger girls. I kept crossing new boundaries. I involved a dog and insects in my sexual rituals.

At twenty-seven, I became involved with a younger woman. My sexual desire knew no limits. I always wanted more, but the more I got, the emptier I felt. After less than a year in this relationship, my mental and physical health deteriorated to the point where I suffered a nervous breakdown. It took three years and therapy for me to recover my health.

It was about that time that I got married. In spite of my best intentions, marriage only gave new impetus to my addiction. Most of my problems reside in my inability to relate to other people, so living with a spouse day-in-and-day-out was impossible for me. The mental escape of acting out was the only way I could cope with the ups and downs of married life.

Four years into our marriage, we were expecting our first child. One night, after one of those horrendous arguments that left us both in the depths of despair, my wife lamented, "Why are we bringing a child into the midst of such chaos and pain?" When my daughter was born, I vowed never to act out around her. Yet only a few years later she walked into the room where I was acting out.

Sex with self was also the way I handled the stresses of my career. It seemed on the surface as if all was going well. I was singled out for my professional achievements and chosen for a management position. Soon I was not only violating the personal space of the people I worked with, but also masturbating at work. For the first time, at age forty, I was sexually inappropriate around two minors in the workplace. My compulsion had progressed to where I was now willing to put my career, reputation, and family at risk. I didn't even consider the legal consequences.

In desperation I decided to change careers, and my wife and I both enrolled in seminary. I sought to avoid my former behaviors with all the willpower I could muster. I thought I had hit bottom. But without a program and a fellowship for monitoring and support, my resolution to change couldn't last. It was during my first year of studies that I had the experience I related at the beginning of my story.

Some time later I talked to a graduate student in the school of psychology about my acting out. She suggested that I go to Sexaholics Anonymous. Six months later, I finally attended my first SA meeting, to check it out. Although I immediately realized I was with people who were just like me, I was still unwilling to accept that I was a sexaholic. I bought a copy of *Sexaholics Anonymous* and started reading it.

Another year went by. After another argument, my wife took the children and left me. Overcome with frustration and anger, I acted out. Once again I found myself tumbling into the abyss of pleasure and pain that had almost engulfed me three years earlier. This time I knew enough to seek out an SA meeting. That was in 1993.

I attended several meetings and then asked an old-timer to be my sponsor. He instructed me to attend meetings where members were working the Steps and getting sober. He told me that SA was going to have to be first in my life. Although I still felt resistance in myself to committing to the program, I started working the Steps under his direction, using *Sexaholics Anonymous, Twelve Steps and Twelve Traditions,* and *Alcoholics Anonymous.* I began to change.

My first reading of *Sexaholics Anonymous* helped me see that I was a sexaholic and could not stay sober by myself. It helped me understand that lust was the driving force behind all of my acting out and that "progressive victory over lust" was the only way to freedom. I had been trying to stop my compulsive behaviors, but they were only symptomatic of my real problem—lust! Finally, it taught me that I could not live in the snake pit of resentment.

In the *Twelve Steps and Twelve Traditions,* the chapter on Step One made it clear to me that I must begin my recovery by accepting my "devastating weakness and all its consequences." It helped me see that if I took hold of the program of Sexaholics Anonymous as a drowning person takes hold of a life preserver, I could get well. The chapter on Step Two solved the riddle of why I was "full of faith" in God, but still "reeking" of lust: I had yet to clean house so that God could enter and drive out the obsession. It convinced me that I could never stay sober unless I stopped placing unreasonable expectations upon myself, others, and God.

Alcoholics Anonymous gave me the Twelve Steps in a simple, straightforward manner that, with the help of my sponsor, I could follow into sober living. It taught me that the first step of recovery was to fully acknowledge that I was a sexaholic. I could not masturbate, entertain lustful thoughts, or practice lustful behaviors without being destroyed by them. It relieved me of my "victim" mentality. My troubles were of my own making, caused by my self-centeredness, not by what others had done to me.

In my early recovery, several experiences stand out for me. One involved playing catch with my seven-year old son. I was at a pool party where there were several attractive women, and I was distracted by lust. My son became flustered and blurted out, "Daddy, why do you keep looking around! Why don't you just play catch with me?" What could I say?

Another time I was at soccer practice with my eleven-year-old daughter. The coach asked me to help tie on the vests that distinguish one team from the other. I suddenly felt a wave of lust for the girl I was assisting. She must have felt the negative psychic energy, for she turned around to face me and gave me an awful, startled look, as if to say, "What *is* your problem?"

In time, I also became aware of the presence of lust in my marriage. I had to give up any expectation of sex with my wife. Sustained periods of abstinence have helped me learn to relate to her without making sex a condition for my love. Our White Book tells me that sex is optional. I know now that this applies not only to sex with myself but also to sex with my wife. True sexual intimacy is based on our freely giving our spirits, hearts, minds, and bodies to each other. If either of us can't live without demanding sex, how can it be the gift of love God intended it to be? Today my wife knows that my love for her is not based on whether or how often she is willing to have sex with me.

In my experience there is no magical path to progressive victory over lust. It is a freedom that comes gradually as I grow spiritually by practicing the Twelve Steps in everyday life. When I am tempted by lust, I turn to the Steps and God for help. For example, I found myself looking at a book on childbirth that was on my daughter's nightstand. It was my daughter's comment, "Gee, Daddy, you sure like that book," that woke me up to the fact that my motive for looking at the book was lustful. I talked about the incident with my sponsor, other members in the program, and in meetings. I admitted I was powerless over that book and turned my choice to look at it over to God. I haven't picked up the book since.

Some months later adversity came my way: I had to report myself to state authorities because of the acting out I did around my daughter years before. Our children were interviewed at their schools by a social worker. My acting out was described to my daughter. When the social worker asked my daughter how she felt about me after hearing about what I'd done, she responded, "I feel pretty weird, but I love my Daddy!" The first part of her response is a direct result of my years of acting out. The latter part I owe to God working through Sexaholics Anonymous to help me become the kind of dad I always wanted to be.

My wife and daughter had to see another social worker to determine what treatment our daughter needed, if any. I underwent the forensic evaluation that all sex offenders undergo in my state. Normally, a person in my situation is removed from his home and is not allowed any contact with his children for a certain period of time. The investigating social worker made a rare exception in our case. She said she did so in part because of our daughter. She came away from their interview convinced that anyone who was raising a daughter like ours must be doing some things right. With my friends in the program and the Steps to guide me, I have come through this adversity sober. It has strengthened my faith.

One day, out of my heart, a plea went up to God, saying, "There must be some useful purpose, some other work you want me to do besides supporting my immediate family." Minutes later I got a telephone call from a person in SA asking me if I would be interested in doing prison service work. I couldn't believe it! I knew it was the "next right thing" God wanted me to do. I have since become involved in writing to inmates, sending out literature to them, and sponsoring an SA group in prison. I also guide and encourage other members who want to do similar service work. I have been given a new purpose in life. Thank God for Sexaholics Anonymous!

13. Sober on the Inside

I am in prison for having sex with a male minor, his brother, and their cousin. The prosecutors had offered me an eight-year sentence on a plea bargain; they told me if I didn't take that, they would try me as a habitual offender and ask for the life sentence. I refused the plea bargain and got the life sentence. Am I mad at myself for being stupid? No! If I had taken the eight years I would have returned to the outside world and to the exact same behavior.

This is my story about how I was able to get sexually sober in prison. It did not happen quickly. In fact, I had served more than eight years before I even woke up to the fact that I had a personal problem. Even then I did not start working on it for another year.

After I had served nine years in prison, I was lucky enough to get help starting the first SA group in any state prison system. Our group got started after I went to the chaplain in our prison. He agreed with me that we needed an SA group. I wrote to SA and explained that we didn't have any money. In response, we received some SA manuals at no cost.

This was in 1984, before it was acceptable to reach out and help sex offenders. Sex offenders as a whole are the most despised people in prison, not only by other prisoners, but also by a lot of the officials. However, the chaplain went to bat for us and was granted permission by our warden for us to meet as long as the chaplain was willing to be our institutional sponsor and to attend our meetings. The chaplain asked that we be willing to meet on our own time and not take time from work. He wanted people who were willing to spend their personal time to get well. He also asked that the parole board not be told about our participation in the meeting, because he didn't want people coming who were only trying to impress the parole board.

Everyone in our group was in prison for a sex crime. At first we usually found our members by sharing one-on-one. Later some of us told our personal counselors that we had a program going. If someone wanted to change, he could ask for an interview with our prison sponsor. The sponsor would then bring the name before the group and we would vote on the person. This way we were able to maintain an ongoing group. We never turned anyone down. We felt that if anyone was looking for help, we were required to hold out a helping hand. This approach worked very well for us.

In our SA group we stressed that it was very important that no one talk with other inmates in the prison about what was said during our meetings. We were very lucky over all the years the group existed. God looked out for us, and none of those who dropped out of our group gossiped about people in the group. This alone showed me that our Higher Power was working for us.

This is how the program worked for us:

> *Meetings.* Our meetings followed a monthly schedule. The first week of the month we did a Step—Step One in January, Step Two in February, etc. The second and third weeks we heard someone's story. The fourth week was usually a tape. If there was a fifth week, we had outside visitors share how they were working the program. We started our meetings with some form of devotion and ended them with the Serenity Prayer.

> *Fellowship.* Even though we all had different types of addictive behavior, we were always able to share our hopes and our ways of overcoming our addiction. I have found that people who are sincere about wanting help are not going to throw stones at other people who have different behaviors. There were people with different forms of sex addiction, but we didn't judge one another. We all shared one thing: the sincere wish to overcome our addiction and to learn to lead a productive life by staying away from things that caused us to come to places like this. Many of us found that we had, for the first time in our lives, found people who truly understood our problems.

Daily program work. Most of the group members knew that to succeed, they would have to work the program every day. I have to start each day with the Steps, and I remind myself how I ended up here in prison. Believe me, I am the only reason I am here! I lied to myself for over forty years, and I can't correct overnight what took years to develop, so I have a lot of work to do each sober day. I have watched people drop out of the program declaring that they are cured, only to return to their old ways. I know that for myself there is no cure, only working the SA program one day at a time.

Step work. I have worked so many things out through the Twelve Steps. I do daily Step work in addition to the Step work done in meetings. We were not able to have Step sponsors or to be Step sponsors for each other, but the group sponsor (the chaplain at first) was able to help all of us.

Honesty. The hardest part of this program for me was to learn to stop lying to myself and to face the fact that I need a lot of help to be restored to sanity. I still have a long way to go, but at least I know that SA and my Higher Power are there to help me find my way. This is very important to me. The fact that after all the years of lying to myself I was able to get honest and to stay honest should show other people that it can be done. I am not saying that it is easy; I am saying that for me it was worth all the effort I put into the program. I sincerely wish I could have been honest years ago, but I was not ready. Now that I am inside, I hope that other people can learn from my mistakes and that maybe I can be a reason for them to change in time to find a productive and happy life. We told new members that the first time through their moral inventory, they would not get completely honest. Some of us had been lying to ourselves for decades (over forty years in my case). We told them to get as honest as they could and then rework their moral inventory a second time. We found that about the third or fourth time, they began to be able to be truly honest. There were a few who could not get honest with the group or themselves. It was sad, but again we knew that this would be the case for some people.

Gratitude. It may sound strange for someone who was sentenced to a life term to tell you he is grateful, but I am grateful just being sober. It is not always easy to stay sober in prison. I am happy that my Higher Power has given me the strength to stay sober. Other group members, who have been released from prison and are living productive, happy lives, have even more reason for gratitude. As far as we know, everyone who got out of prison from our group has been able to stay out! This has been a very important morale booster for the rest of us.

Service work. I am not a well-educated person, but I believe that I can give moral support to other people who are honestly trying to find a way to change and to live productive, happy lives.

Outside contact. Our group was fortunate to have contact with some SA members from the outside who came to our prison to share their stories. Most of us in the group were doing long sentences, and we were all interested in learning more about how other members stay sober. Over the years several members of the SA Correctional Facilities Committee (SACFC) have visited me and helped me stay sober by moving forward with my program. The SA members who do prison service work are all needed and are important in getting programs started. Those who go into prisons help people on the inside by showing them ways they can stay sober. We need sincere people to visit us who understand that we are sincerely looking for ways to become sober.

Now I want to tell you about some attitude adjustments that I, personally, have had to make:

> *Victim stance.* It is very easy to get into the habit of blaming my weakness and my difficulties on other people. I will not recover until I face my Higher Power and accept that I did make a lot of bad choices in my life. I have to do better. My own actions are the reason I am here.

> *Self-centeredness.* Most people who end up in prison for sex offenses are very self-centered people. I cannot have friends if I cannot be a friend. How could I ever have any kind of relationship before, when my whole life was all about myself? I was so tied up in self-satisfaction that I never had time to care about anyone else. Although sex ruled my life completely, I still told myself that I didn't have any problem. That stinking thinking led me to this place.

> *Progression.* I know from experience that my addiction gets progressively worse each year that it isn't reversed. Without help, I can easily turn down a very dangerous path. Looking at the course of my life, I can get depressed at times. But if I take a few minutes to seek God's advice, He lifts my spirits and shows me the right way to go. I must always remember that I should not do anything without seeking His advice.

> *No cure.* I do not believe that I will ever completely overcome my sexual problems. Some people work the program for a short while and then believe that they no longer need it. It is not very long before they find themselves slipping back into their old ways. I am not looking for a way to be cured. I am quite content to keep working the Twelve Steps one day at a time.

Our prison group helped me to get sober in 1987 and to stay sober. The group lasted over twelve years, and then the state shut it down. Not too long after that, three members of the SA Correctional Facilities Committee visited me. They asked me to write my story and also to write letters to other inmates and talk about my road of recovery. I almost said no, because I was such a poor letter writer. But my Higher Power said yes, and told me to get busy. For the next nine years, all my Twelve Step and SA work was done by mail. At one point, I was writing to over twenty-five inmates. That took over my whole life. A very good and sober life it turned out to be!

Once again, the state stepped in and said that inmates could not write other inmates unless they were related. Now what could my Higher Power do about that? The next thing I knew, the authorities did a special review of my record and granted parole! I'm expecting release within four to eight months as I write.

People who are really seeking to get sober and recover from their addiction will go to any length to get and keep the program. This will not happen overnight, but I do believe that as long as we have people like the Correctional Facilities Committee of Sexaholics Anonymous helping us, we will be able to overcome setbacks. It is through our Higher Power that we band together and reach out to help one another learn to stay sober.

14. A Deluge of Grace

On a long holiday weekend, I was finishing my third hour in a porno shop. Finally someone entered my viewing booth to act out with me. That was the last time I had sex with another and the beginning of understanding how the lust drug had polluted my soul. I had spent the three-day weekend in almost total obsession, but now the trance ended. The smell, the dirt on the walls, the peepholes, the degradation of myself and another human being—all this overwhelmed me with waves of shame and self-hate. Only a deluge of grace could free me.

I was an only child. When I was eight years old, my twenty-nine-year-old mother died suddenly of a heart attack. After that I lived with my father and his eighty-year-old mother.

My father was often absent, drinking. Once, in my early teens, when he came home drunk in the middle of the night, I physically and verbally abused him and disowned him as my father. Resentment had turned to rage.

The summer when I was eleven, a friend's older brother initiated us into masturbation. The practice took root with a vengeance. I had found my outlet for rage, pain, and loneliness. It became daily and compulsive, with the added excitement of risking discovery in the classroom and other public places.

As I entered high school, my self-hatred grew. Shame pervaded my very being. My idol from grade school was now a popular athlete, handsome and spiritually inclined. Because he was my friend, I felt worthwhile. I carried this pattern of getting my worth from dependent male friendships into adult life.

When I was a sophomore in high school, several events converged to bring about a religious conversion in my life. I drank my first hard liquor at a New Year's Eve party and passed out. In fear of the disease that killed my grandfather and was destroying my father and uncle, I resolved to stop drinking.

Two weeks later a friend with whom I had carried newspapers was killed. I determined to be like him, a spiritual person. Soon after this, I went to a retreat led by a former World War II chaplain who now worked with prisoners. Instead of rejecting me, he radiated love as I confessed the sins of my life up to that point. This first Step Five experience helped me believe that God is a God of love and compassion. I started to believe that I could count on Him in my struggles with lust and life. Following the directions of this priest, I began to go to Mass daily and to examine my conscience regularly. I found a spiritual director whom I saw weekly. I was open with him about every aspect of my life and sexuality.

I entered into an extended period of sexual abstinence. I began to expand my network of friends. My sense of self worth grew. I began to dream of doing for others what had been done for me through those who publicly gave their lives to God.

I graduated from high school. With great relief, I left home to begin the adventure of entering a religious community. There was intensive spiritual training with much structure and discipline. Masturbation was not a part of my life. Lustful literature was not available, nor was alcohol. However, there was a romanticized, idealized male relationship that fed my lust.

After four years of this protected environment, I went from the country to the city to study for my degree. Alcohol was available. I began to drink, and soon I began to masturbate again. Within days I was into compulsive masturbation, soon with objects. I initiated sex with classmates. I wanted to be lusted after; I became a tease.

Three years after I was ordained, the pressure of the public role and the split between my secret actions and that public role created unbearable stress. I numbed myself with more masturbation and infatuation. In the midst of an extended crisis in the institution where I was working, I went into a three-week manic high, which resulted in a month of psychiatric hospitalization.

After that, my addiction intensified. In a postgraduate sexuality class, photographs of hard-core pornography were made available as exhibits. Again and again I returned to view the photos. The fire was lit. A number of years after this, I went into a porn shop for the first time in a city some distance from my own. A conflagration took place within me: the forbidden, the dangerous—and *moving* pictures! I went especially for same-sex pornography; it excited my lust more intensely.

I determined I would never go into a porn place in my home town. Within a year I crossed that boundary. The danger of discovery and recognition fueled the fire. The next boundary I crossed was in the city where I grew up. For the first time I propositioned a man in a dangerous part of town. I was unsuccessful and was pursued by two cars full of men ready for violence. Fleeing to safe territory, I totaled my car in another part of town. A lawyer friend of a friend took care of this for me long distance. Another decade of progressive addiction was yet to come.

All this time, on the outside I was a successful church leader, but frustration, loneliness, and self-pity were driving me ever deeper into the fix of my secret life. Coworkers had challenged me about angry outbursts toward authority figures at staff meetings. I tried the geographic cure. I moved a long distance away to an isolated part of the country. I curtailed drinking. Acting out with others and self seemed to recede, but intoxicated anger (without alcohol) gradually increased.

When I traveled, my lust took over. Voyeurism, exhibitionism—I would leave for three days of rest and return hung over from a three-day binge fed by rest stops, malls, and cruising areas. The terrifying realization came that all of this was occurring without alcohol! Alcohol had been my cover for twenty years. I could always blame it on having "one too many." Now "it" had a life of its own apart from alcohol. Lust obsession without alcohol progressed for three more years.

After the incident in the porno shop, my superiors sent me to an urban area where there were more resources. My closest friend lived there, one of the friendships in my life that I had not sexualized. I had always told myself that when I was with someone I really cared about, who knew me and I knew him, that I never had any problem. After two weeks, I was into voyeurism and cruising in a local mall.

A key delusion was now dead: no one, no matter how good, how caring, how loving—no friendship, no matter how significant in my life—could enable me to control lust. Indeed, lust was slowly eating away at my capacity to relate on any level with those who really cared for me.

I went to a city where I knew there were Twelve-Step groups and other resources for sexual recovery. Someone told me there was a fellow trying to start an SA group. I called the number given me. "Is it true?" I asked. "Sure," he replied. "We need you; show up tomorrow night. I can't be there, but the others will be." I went and found three others. Two months earlier one of the fellowship's old-timers had carried the message to this area. This was the fourth meeting of SA since that visit. I was home. I felt safe. Since that day in 1983, I have not found it necessary to act out.

During my first year in the program, I attended five to seven meetings a week and spent hours with my sponsors and other re-covering members. My sponsor, over two years sober, assured me that a day would come when I would be able to begin to tell the difference between "chemistry" and authentic intimacy.

As I detoxed from my lust and acting out, the depth of the dis-ease hit me. My powerlessness went beyond anything I could have imagined. One day, while taking my daily walk, I became con-scious that I was scanning both sides of a busy street for lust ob-jects. This was an automatic gear that my brain shifted into in cer-tain public places. Shame would start to take over. It seemed, sometimes, that my first impulse toward every person, place, and feeling was lust; my second was shame. I came to call the im-pulses of lust and shame the arthritis of my soul. Until I accepted them in the spirit of the First Step, I was not ready to ask for and receive the comfort and strength of my Higher Power.

Six months into sobriety, forty-one years after my mother's death, I tapped the buried grief. For over an hour, tears rose. I ex-perienced healing and freedom.

I discovered that just as I had pockets of shame, I had hidden pockets of unbelief. I was praying one early winter morning on my way to a meeting while I was in the midst of my Fourth Step. I was telling God how much I believed He cared for me from the first moment of my conception. I paused for a red light. In the silence I heard the wordless response, "Yes, but you don't believe for one minute that I can free you from your slavery to lust." A light went on in my soul. A burden lifted. I was freed to take the next Step.

I reconnected with the remnants of my mother's family and reached out in gratitude to those men who had been significant mentors in my past life. I made conscious, intentional space for friendship, especially for the friend who had been with me after my last acting out and helped me make the decision to go to any lengths for recovery. His friendship represents forty-five years of faithful, caring presence in my life. In sobriety our friendship has grown from one of dependence to one of mutual respect and sharing. I have been open with my religious community about my addiction. Their support and affirmation of my recovery have been a constant source of strength.

I have discovered that sex is indeed optional. I experience celibacy as a way to express my faith and love in the service of others. Living this lifestyle gives me joy and freedom. It is a special gift to be with sober married men who choose times of extended sexual abstinence for the sake of healing in their marriage relationships.

My sobriety has been constantly deepened by the many opportunities I have had to carry the message of my recovery. The wonder of what has happened to me is renewed and my heart is filled with joy when someone is willing to listen to my story. I thank God for all of those who have given me this gift.

After my first year in recovery I started a significant research and writing project. During this time, I risked true friendship with a woman. She was an artist who drew out the artist in me. I began to paint and write poetry. She awakened in me feelings I had never expected to experience. Wise mentors kept me from running away, from obsessing on the theme: if she only knew! "Go slowly," they said, "not all at once." "Stay in the present." "Don't let shame dump your story on her. Wait for the right time. You will know." I had grown enough to surrender my shame fits and follow their counsel of loving patience. My friendship with her blossomed, and she has become a cherished part of my life.

Ten years into recovery I received a surprising phone call from my superior, who knew my story. I was asked to present myself for an office of major responsibility and trust. I had been a marginal performer. Now I was being asked to take a most sensitive position of trust, doing work for which absolutely everything in my life up to this time helped prepare me. My sponsor and friends who knew my story supported me in this. They told me, "You are the one."

I am now in my sixth year in this position. It has not been easy, even with all the support I have received; yet I am growing and happy. My sponsor has challenged me to new levels of surrender in finally accepting that my depressive episodes and periodic highs do indicate that I have a chemical imbalance which is carried by three generations of males on my mother's side of the family. After three years of resisting, I am following my doctor's suggestions.

My inclination to play God in other people's lives, trying to fix and control them, created a second bottom in my recovery. I became enmeshed with some of those I was helping professionally or as a sponsor. The pain of these struggles with relationships drove me to seek help from S-Anon and other resources. Now, with sponsorship and professional supervision, I am growing in my ability to keep appropriate boundaries.

My resentment toward religious authority and institutions still flares up and even infects my relationship with my sponsor. Any authority will do! When I follow his suggestion to make a gratitude list for all my religious tradition has given to me personally and to the world, when I am willing to inventory my resentment and share it, when I am willing to humbly ask God to remove what I cannot, then I know the newness of stepping into adulthood.

A few years ago I moved to the city in which I am now working. I had decided not to start an SA group. Too many things to do! God had other plans. Within two months, He sent me two fellows in incredible pain. I wasn't too interested in sponsoring anyone at that time. I said, "Call me tomorrow if you want to stay sober another day." I wasn't expecting that to go on for long.

They started calling and kept calling, and they stayed sober! These two renewed my stagnated program. They asked me to repeat the questions I asked them the day before. "What questions?" I said. "The ones about desiring sobriety," they replied. Out of this evolved the practice of renewing each day our desire for sobriety. We asked each other, "Can you admit you are powerless over lust? Do you desire sobriety for today? Are you willing to protect and strengthen this desire one day at a time?" One day a caller unexpectedly threw a surprise at me: "Are you willing to hand over your will and life, just for today, to the One who kept you sober yesterday *and protected you from the full consequences of your lust in the past?"*

I thought of all the consequences from which I have been spared: arrest and public exposure, beatings and death, AIDS, disappointment of those people who had put their trust in me. Whenever I remember these things, I feel deep gratitude to the One who has cared for me through all these years of insanity.

Although I have been spared the full consequences of my disease, the humiliations have been real and sufficiently painful to drive me into SA. What one of AA's early friends said to a critic of AA surely applies to us: "These fellows have a specialty. Their specialty is humiliations; and they have found the way to change humiliations into humility and thus be readied for a deluge of God's grace."

I have experienced a deluge of grace. I know my true identity in a new way, with conscious awareness and understanding. Always and everywhere, even in the depth of my insanity, I believe I have belonged to a Love from which I came: the God of my good desires, the God of my sobriety.

My sexaholism teaches me that I need you who share my lust addiction so that I do not forget who I am, a beloved child of God.

15. Dependent Me

As a child I was always seeking attention, wanting to be the center of attention. It never worked. And I could never stay still. I was always bouncing on the sofa or on my grandmother's rocking chair.

I have been dependent as long as I can remember. At school, I would sit outside on the steps crying; my sister would sit next to me, assuring me it was alright for me to go in, that Mom would be there at the end of the day. I would lie to the school nurse and get her to call my mother to come get me.

Every time a love story came on television, my sisters would call to me, "Hurry, your favorite story is on!" I was a love addict from the first moment I can remember. I still remember my first kiss, under the table in kindergarten. Oh boy, I was in LOVE!

Then boyfriends, always chasing them. When they chased me I was not interested.

I got involved with drugs and alcohol in my teens. Then, at the age of eighteen, I found the big S word, SEX. I was off and running. From then until I arrived on the steps of SA, I was busy. My favorite thing was to entice and tease. I loved the forbidden. Excitement!

I married for the first time at the age of twenty-four. For the next twelve years I lived in hell, my own, of course; I would act in—obsessing on fantasy and romance—and then act out. Our relationship was all about abuse. He abused me physically and sexually. I stayed right in there! I'd look him in the eye and make sure he kept abusing me. It got worse and worse.

When I started a business, my lust took flight from reality. POWER. I traveled the world, drunk on myself. I would tease and entice the men I met, business contacts, the airline passenger next to me. But in my mind I was saying, "You can't touch me!" I was playing for the intrigue.

I divorced. I thought, "Now I am free!" Yet I could not speak up for myself during the divorce so that even today I pay money monthly to my ex. Talk about powerless!

Then for two years, I would go in and out of relationships, if you could call them that. I would date homosexuals, thinking, "Oh boy, look! They love me and want to change!" As far as I know, they never did.

My disease progressed until I decided, no more sex. Two months later, my second husband came on the scene. I remember thinking that I needn't worry about hearing from him again since I had not given him my home number and, at the office, my secretary would screen the call. That same day he called me at home. "Oh boy," I thought, "this time I'm not the predator—he's the predator!" Now I liked being pursued. Two months later I was living with him. How did that happen? He said, "I will only move in if you marry me." I knew he would not marry a person like me, so I said, "Move in!" Eight months later we were married.

He introduced me to the Twelve Step program of AA. I thought, "How nice!" So I went to Al-Anon and later to AA. This did not slow me down one bit. I stopped drinking alcohol, yet my dependency was growing daily.

Then he walked into SA. I saw a sparkle in his eyes I had never seen before, so I walked in myself to check it out. I attended six meetings and then ran as fast as I could to S-Anon.

My life was going down hill. I was over one hundred thousand dollars in debt, could not work my business, could not travel, and was afraid to do anything. I was dizzy with dependency and compulsive sex. My husband and I separated again and again; each time I would act out with him to get him back. Some of my friends in S-Anon were attending SA meetings, but I avoided talking about it with them.

Then—I remember it so clearly—I awoke in the middle of the night in an absolute panic. I felt empty. I woke a friend and said, "I need to go to SA." We went to a meeting the next day. I knew I belonged—yet again, I thought, "I'm not as bad as these people." After three meetings, I said, "We need to start a women's meeting." We did. It didn't make me sober. I kept coming back, but I could not get sober.

Then one day in 1998 I hit bottom. I knew it was over. I came home, called a local SA member and said, "Could I have your sponsor's phone number?" She gave it to me, and I made the call. Her sponsor asked me one question, "Do you want to stop lusting?" "Yes," I answered. I was defeated.

Now she became my sponsor. I called her every day. I took suggestions. For the next ninety days I attended a meeting every day.

We began to read the SA White Book: I had to tell her what made me a sexaholic. I saw the place that says, "Please connect with me and make me whole!" Also, "First addicts, then love cripples. . . ." Hello!—that was me.

Next we began working the steps in the AA Big Book. My sponsor asked me to read the first 103 pages and then identify how that was me. Oh my goodness, I saw myself! I began to work the Steps.

In Step One, I found out I have a CHOICE. Amazing!

In Step Two, I found out that I wasn't the Higher Power and others were not either.

In Step Three, I had to make a decision: Did I want to do God's will or continue to do mine? When I was ready, I got on my knees with another SA member and turned my will (thoughts) and life (actions) over to God. This Step taught me I have a PURPOSE.

I spent many months writing my Fourth Step inventory, following *Alcoholics Anonymous*, pages 63-71. I wrote down my resentments, and then I did the "turn-arounds," in which I put on paper how I had been selfish, dishonest, self-seeking, and frightened in the situations that prompted my resentments. Though a situation had not been entirely my fault, I tried to disregard the other person's part. Where was I to blame? When I saw my faults, I listed them, admitted them honestly, and became willing to set those matters straight. I did the same kind of exhaustive inventory on my fears and my sexual behavior. This was the first stage to cleaning house. I saw the patterns of my behavior and what part I played in the illness. To complete my sexual inventory, I wrote a letter to God. I asked God to form my sexual attitudes and ideals according to His will and to help me to live up to my ideals. I felt myself beginning to awaken. I was changing.

Step Five was about speaking it out loud to my sponsor and to God. No more secrets. This Step is where I found God.

In Steps Six and Seven, I looked at my emotional sobriety. I saw that the character defects that showed up in Step Four could be removed if I asked God to remove them and then was willing to take the necessary action to be a mature adult.

Steps Eight and Nine will never be finished. I make amends daily by the way I live, and I also continue making amends from my Eighth Step list. Forgiveness and freedom. I'm learning to do the right thing.

I live in Steps Nine, Ten, Eleven, and Twelve. Part of my evening meditation is a constructive review of my day, a Tenth Step inventory in which I identify any actions that need to be corrected or any secrets that need to be brought into the light with another person. In the morning, I try to get myself in the right spiritual attitude for the next twenty-four hours. I ask for direction with the issues of the day. I ask for the intuitive thought or decision that will keep me in God's will.

In addition to the Steps, I also use the Twelve Traditions in my daily life. I have studied the Traditions with a service sponsor, a sober sexaholic with whom I work the Traditions and the Concepts. The Concepts show me how to love the world I live in. The Traditions have been a guide to healthy relationships. My sponsor taught me that I had no idea how to have relationships; I was a relationship junkie. Today, I have many healthy relationships.

I had to face my core issue of dependency in my marriage. Ultimately, my spouse did not choose recovery, and we divorced. I understand today that in order to be in a relationship both parties need to be healthy.

Today I sponsor other women with the sole purpose of taking them through the Twelve Steps, the Twelve Traditions, and the Twelve Concepts. My sponsor asked me, "What did SA give you? Now what are you willing to give to others?" A lot of my time is spent in giving back.

Today, inspired by the first one hundred alcoholics who recovered in AA, I call myself a recovered sexaholic. I am so grateful to our fellowship and to all who came before me and to all who are just beginning the journey. I am grateful to my Higher Power, who brought me into this fellowship of sexaholics.

Dependent me? Now I say, "Dependent on God." That is how it works.

16. Her Father's Daughter

As a child, I lived in a fantasy world. A healthy imagination helps prepare a child for life; but for me, fantasy distorted reality and prepared the way for future confusion and unmanageability.

I was very close to my father. I knew I was the person he loved best in the whole world—more than my mother, more than my brothers, more than anyone else. As a teenager, I felt awkward and phony when I tried to date boys. I found I could not introduce them to my father without feeling deep shame mixed with hostility and contempt. I was frustrated, and I didn't understand why.

Eventually, I decided to join the lesbian community. What a relief. This was me. I had found the place where I belonged. I participated actively. I had many friends and several serious relationships. Yet, I was never quite satisfied. I was always searching for a more desirable partner.

As time passed, my relationships became emotionally painful. I began to hate the drinking that was part of my gay lifestyle. So, ten years after I first joined the lesbian community, I attended my first gay AA meeting. It was a large meeting of about one hundred members in Canada. I was delighted to find so many non-drinking potential partners. I quickly acquired an AA sponsor. She helped me find God. I started praying to the God of my understanding. My sponsor insisted that I write a Fourth Step inventory. I attended a meeting every day for two years. During this time, I would court one lover while living with another.

Finally, the honesty of the Twelve Step program got through to me. I opened up emotionally and began to talk in meetings--about my brothers, my family, my past. I talked so much that some group members felt uncomfortable. As I continued to share, emotions of intense hatred melted away. I developed genuine empathy for my brothers and for fellow AA members.

Then, the unexpected happened. I fell in love with a bisexual man who had AIDS. At the same time, I was also in love with another woman. I was confused. I was terrified. I ran. I moved West more than half a continent away.

There I quickly connected with the lesbian community but did not get involved with anyone. When my female roommate moved out, a male friend of hers moved in for a short stay. He was a recovering member of Sexaholics Anonymous. Upon hearing my story, he became convinced that I was a sexaholic, too. He played tapes of SA members' stories when I was home. He dragged me to an SA meeting. A member there assured me, "You qualify." I did not want to hear it.

I attended SA meetings for about a month, then stopped. It was too scary for me to be in a meeting room full of men. In my mind, men were the enemy, the evildoers of the world. By this time, I understood I was a sexaholic. I admired sober SA members, but I had nightmares about going to SA meetings. I felt I was betraying my friends. I was loath to break my strong bonding and close ties to the lesbian community. I asked myself, "If I go to SA, how can I face the people I belong to?"

I had learned to trust the Twelve Step process. On my own, I began to make amends for the wreckage of my past. I stopped having relationships but continued sex with self and writing pornography. It took me two years to overcome my fear of sitting in the same room with SA men. I then returned to SA and got sober.

After six months of SA sobriety, I came to experience, on a deep level, the reality of Steps One, Two and Three: I can't; God can; so I'll let go and let God. I surrendered not only my lust but also my will and my life to God's loving care. God proved to be a more capable manager than I.

I experienced significant emotional growth during the following years. After I had been sober three years, I realized I had been my father's surrogate spouse from an early age. As part of recovery, I moved beyond this role. As I changed, so did my father. One day he surprised me by announcing his plans to remarry.

Today, my life no longer revolves around relationships. I feel emotionally stable. Before sobriety, I was mentally and emotionally unable to cope with schoolwork. I have now returned to school to earn a Bachelor of Science Degree. I keep my life peaceful and simple. I like to meditate. I focus on God's will for me, one day at a time.

17. God Works through Others

I am a recovering sexaholic. I have been sober since 1984.

It is hard to say exactly when my sexaholism began. I started masturbating in my high-school years, and pornography was almost immediately a part of that experience. From the very beginning, the pornography-masturbation ritual was a two-edged sword. I got a tremendous high not only from the pornography, but also from the secrecy, the anticipation, and the buildup. I was addicted to it. There was also a tremendous guilt, shame, and loneliness that followed every experience.

In college I discovered adult bookstores. I had been to X-rated movies, but this was different. I felt like a kid in a candy store. The options seemed unlimited—and a private booth to boot! From the very first time, the candy-store illusion was unmasked when I noticed someone staring at me from above my "private" booth. Being from a conservative religious background, such an experience would normally have kept me away for good. My lust for the experience kept me going back, despite other moments of fear and danger. Most of my acting out was in such places.

I was one year out of college and teaching when I got involved in an affair with a married woman. While there were certainly honest feelings of affection for each other, there was also lust. I was also drinking alcoholically, and I seemed unable to stop the affair. I was depressed and drunk and awash in a sea of shame and despair. I stopped for two months, realized I no longer loved this woman, and decided to end the affair. On the last day of school, when she asked if I still loved her, I lied and had sex with her. It was a devastating moment in my life.

A few months later I got sober from alcohol. For two months, although I did not stop all masturbation, I stayed out of bookstores and porno theaters. I felt that the sexual acting out had been part of my alcoholism and that I was now free of it. Then, on a trip to a large city, I discovered bookstores with "live" women in them. Lust was off and running in me for another two and a half years. I became increasingly unable to stay away from places of pornography despite prayer and other efforts to do so. I was hooked. This became most clear to me on two occasions. First, I drove by a bookstore I didn't know existed. The adrenalin and the ritual began immediately. I prayed that I wouldn't stop the car. I stopped it. I prayed that I wouldn't get out of the car. I got out. I prayed that I wouldn't go in. I went in. I prayed that I wouldn't masturbate. Needless to say, I did.

Second, I was in a bookstore with "live" dancers and experiencing an intense high. The dancers changed shifts in the middle of my experience. The lack of reality and the phoniness of the connection overwhelmed me. Driving home, I tried to soothe myself with the thought, "I'm only human." A few seconds later, I found myself pulled over to the side of the road, pounding the steering wheel and screaming in rage and shame at having failed again.

The first person to tell me this problem might be an addiction was the woman who is today my wife. I told her about my experiences, and she said it reminded her of my drinking. I calmly explained to her that the two had nothing to do with each other. I continued acting out, but the seed had been planted. Later my brother began calling me and telling me about his problems with acting out. He was looking for a way to stop. I told him nothing of my own experiences and listened in real fear for us both as I played the role of observant advisor. One night I ended up in a place where pornography led into prostitution. I remember the rage and shame I felt as a stranger kissed me on the cheek and quoted prices. I also remember the intense lust that I felt. This was a moment of truth for me. The lust and shame cycle was so intense that I might never stop.

I talked to my brother and told him the truth: "I've been doing the same thing you have." I burst into tears and asked for help. He had found a Twelve-Step fellowship for sex addiction, and I began to attend also. (This was not SA but another of the S-programs.) At last I found a place I could tell the truth about my lonely secret. What I heard shocked me. Many members were worse off than I was! I resented having to be with such perverts, but I knew that I, too, had perverted my sexuality. So, though angry, I stayed. By the second meeting, I was staying sober! For me this meant no masturbation and no sex except with my fiancée. (Members of this program set their own definitions of sobriety.)

For the next three years I attended this fellowship regularly. I met wonderful people and got help to stay sober. I got a sponsor and worked the Steps, especially the housecleaning Steps, Four through Nine. I married the woman who had stood with me through the worst of my alcoholism and sexaholism. My life was improving, but I began to get uncomfortable at the meetings. The many differences in what constituted sobriety seemed to lead to situations where one member struggled to stop doing something someone else was doing and reporting as sober behavior. I was concerned about unity of purpose. I began to feel I was staying sober almost in spite of the conflicts in the group.

Once again my brother led me deeper into the solution. He had started an SA meeting which I began to attend. SA became my primary group as I sadly said goodbye to my first S-fellowship. SA was different and more rigorous. There were many debates about the sobriety statement, but I knew I had found a home for myself, so I kept coming back.

My early recovery was filled with a lot of behaviors designed to reduce temptation. Don't take the second look, don't drive down that street, keep your eyes on the sidewalk. I said frequent prayers of surrender. I used the phone frequently. I turned over lustful thoughts and images. I stopped going to R-rated movies. I cut back on TV. I kept to a minimum relationships with women other than my wife, family, and established friends. I began to do service work with others. In a few years, I attended my first international convention; I have missed few since. There I see greater lengths and greater quality of sobriety in larger numbers than in my home city. People I have met there have become lifelong friends. Involvement in these conventions has become a key ingredient in my continued sobriety.

My marriage has gotten better and better. Through both a voluntary and an involuntary abstinence period, my wife and I have cleared out much of the lust in our sexual history. I have learned that sex is truly optional. Through our deepening intimacy, both emotional and sexual, we have learned what works for us in terms of both the importance and the limits of sex within the marriage. We have done an entire historical sexual inventory of our marriage and benefited greatly from the process. Recently I made new commitments in the area of language use and household tasks that are further strengthening our growing bond. It was in my wife's father's death and in the loss of a child through miscarriage that I finally knew for sure that I truly love her. We now have two beautiful children who, God willing, will never have an active sexaholic for a father. My family will reap the benefits of the true sexuality that recovery is giving us over time.

SA alone has not answered all my problems. I take help wherever I can get it. I am involved in another Twelve-Step fellowship. I meet regularly with a psychologist. I am active in my church. But SA is the foundation of my sexual sobriety. It is Twelfth Step work that has most benefited my recovery. Service at the national level and in helping to plan an international convention has helped me to grow, and I've made great friends. Recently my service has focused on sponsorship. I cannot begin to describe the joy I receive in opening myself up to the newcomer and to those struggling to maintain sobriety. It has taken me out of much of my arrogance, intolerance, and rigidity and has made me feel more truly connected with God and the fellowship than ever before. Most of all, it has helped me to maintain my own sobriety during some troubling times. I truly need my sponsees more than they need me.

I have said little about God. Some of that is by design. I'm not that comfortable using God's name for fear of being glib and easy about it. I can only say that I believe that God works through others and that God has given me a beautiful fellowship of the most unlikely friends, who have loved me and through whom God continues to work in marvelous ways. To my God and my friends in recovery I say, "Thank you!"

18. Breaking Out of Isolation

I am a woman who was Twelfth-Stepped by a "Dear Abby" column about sex addiction. When I read the word "sexaholic," I knew it described me. This was what I was, how I behaved. I knew that no matter what the cost or how great my fear, I had to break out of my isolation and find the fellowship that the columnist described. Since then, my Higher Power has given me more opportunities to break out of my isolation and choose recovery over self-will.

I lost my home group before I was two years sober. My Higher Power saw fit to move me to a remote area of my state. Friends encouraged me to trust and to stay close with the telephone. My fear was almost more than I could bear, but I saw that a door had opened. I would walk in faith to the other side.

Thank goodness, I found another sex addiction fellowship! I was home—or so I thought. The controlling sexaholic in me took charge of the meetings. No more namby-pamby sobriety—mine was the "real deal." I believed that our SA fellowship was the only one for the true sexaholic, those "who have lost their legs" and cannot grow new ones, as *Alcoholics Anonymous* describes it. The curious and the uncommitted fell away. Fortunately, I found a woman in the group who sponsored me and taught me about the origin of this disease, the feelings we have that we try to cover up. She helped me to accept my womanliness and my body. All were rewarding lessons, but after a time, it happened again—no group. I was alone.

What was I to do? I had been "willing to go to any length," or so I thought. I realized, however, that over the years I had made excuses for missing the SA international conventions. No money and no time—or was it no time and no money? I had even registered early for one convention, agreed to chair a meeting, and then backed out at the last minute with a "headache"—really, a term paper. But now my back was against the wall. I felt very isolated.

I received a notice for a convention with the title, "Free at Last"—nearly identical to the phrase used in the headline for the "Dear Abby" column. That caught my attention. I felt the need to be with SA people. So, still feeling isolated, I went. The convention weekend brought a reawakening of my program. I felt united again with the people who had helped me to get sober and keep sober. I felt the real Connection.

Things began to change. I was invited to lead an SA spring retreat with another SA woman. No more solo recovery or running the show. The experience prepared me for a major surrender: I failed a critical exam in my university program. I no longer had the crutch of school—or even a career. My life was in flux. I was not in control. On the day I was preparing to move again, this time to the West Coast to live for a time with my father, Central Office called with an invitation to serve on an SA service committee. Three weeks later, I was in Los Angeles with old friends and new.

I settled in with my father, surrounded now by members of my family of origin. I needed to learn to live as one among many in my family and to make amends for wrongs I had committed against them. I accepted my powerlessness over the addiction in all its forms. The sickness and dependency that I saw among family members gave me the opportunity to learn detachment at a deeper level.

My longing for a relationship gave me another opportunity to surrender. In fury and sorrow I turned to God and gave it up to Him. Sobriety has required me to discipline myself and, at times, to experience profound loneliness. I used to believe that if only I had a relationship, I would not suffer so. Today I believe that the crying out of the soul to God is part of the fundamental truth of our experience as recovering sexaholics, which we can only experience by forgoing the misplaced love we seek to give or receive. I am grateful for the Steps, and especially to my sponsor, who helped me break free of my isolation. I came to believe in the wisdom of avoiding relationships for a time. As a single sexaholic, I doubt I could have maintained my sobriety had I tried it my way. In time, I began to enjoy my solitude. I learned to be nurturing to myself when I have feelings of being unloved and unacceptable. I became a person I respect and even love. I tried to express this love to others unconditionally. When I was ready, I found a man with whom I could share my life, and I am now learning to live my recovery program in a marriage relationship.

Fear has been the greatest scourge of my recovery, fear that the lust would overtake me, fear of others, and fear of others' lust. Today I need never return to the bondage and the isolation my illness inflicted upon me. This requires surrendering lust on a daily basis, going to SA meetings regularly, attending international conventions and retreats, making myself available for service work, reaching out to other recovering sexaholics, and letting go of old ideas. Sober now since 1983, the most important lesson I have learned is to give myself the privilege and experience of a strong, sound fellowship, a channel whereby God works in my life.

19. Finding Recovery that Fits

Before I came into Sexaholics Anonymous, I did a lot of hard soul-searching. At the time, I was working the Twelve Steps in recovery from alcoholism and considered myself to be relatively safe from the dangers of other addictions. I was in ignorance of the cunning, baffling and powerful nature of sexaholism and in denial about the extent of my lust obsession.

My denial of my sick sexual behavior followed the pattern of my earlier denial of alcoholism. I didn't see how I could live a normal life without drinking. As long as I could control it, I thought, I had a chance to beat it. For years, I struggled under the lash of alcohol addiction. During that time, my drinking masked my sexual addiction and confused those who tried to help me.

I started drinking in my late teens, mostly to relieve inhibitions I had with girls my age. I had been acting out sexually since I was fourteen, having discovered masturbation while trying to steal sex from my sister in her sleep. My pursuit of sex caused a split in my relations with God, my family, and my peers. It's either God or masturbation, my religion seemed to say, and I chose masturbation. Since age ten or eleven, I had been "acting in," entertaining fantasies of romance and sex in order to escape a fear-filled family atmosphere. In school, I spent a lot of time looking forward to the day when I could escape geographically.

When I did move from home, instead of becoming self-sufficient as I had planned and dreamed, I began to drink heavily. People sometimes told me I should watch my drinking. No one confronted me about my sexual pursuits; either they didn't know about them or didn't consider them to be harmful. Pursuing sex and relationships seemed to be keeping me active socially while alcohol gave me something to blame if I made a fool of myself trying to connect.

My life changed when I got a job that gave me security and a future. For the first time I tried to stop drinking. I decided the real problem was the anxiety I felt when I wasn't drinking, and I resolved to address that. But when I talked to professionals, I was careful not to mention my excessive drinking lest they think I was an alcoholic. To get my drinking under control I'd have to treat the anxiety. Stopping drinking wasn't on my agenda.

Eventually my health gave out, and I decided to give up drinking on my doctor's recommendation. This lasted for nine months, at which time I decided to try some controlled drinking. I tried to set limits on myself, carefully avoiding old haunts, but it wasn't long before the old patterns came back. I would stash bottles in my apartment, even though I was living by myself! One morning I woke up sick and decided to take my doctor's advice and go to AA.

The AA fellowship had an immediate, profound effect on me, even from my first meeting. It was the first time ever that I had sat among a group of truly diverse people who helped each other to solve a common problem that they couldn't solve alone. No last names and no keeping tabs on attendance. No authority figures monitoring the proceedings. No rationalizing or making excuses when it came to talking about drinking. And people were using a word to describe themselves that I thought I could never get past my lips: alcoholic. As soon as I admitted it, however—as soon as I identified myself as an alcoholic—my life changed for the better.

The effects were immediate and dramatic. It was true I had the problem, but now I had the solution, too. I had something concrete I could work on. For the first time in a long time I didn't feel crazy. I had a primary purpose, something I could live up to. I stopped feeling lonely. I learned I could abstain from drinking for one day. As a drinker I was no stranger to the day-at-a-time way of life, telling myself for years, "I'll quit tomorrow." Now I could apply the same formula to the solution.

Before AA, I didn't believe in powerlessness and consequently had the concept of recovery back to front. I wanted to solve my problems so that I could try controlled drinking. In retrospect, it was as though I was willing to work all the Steps except the First. But AA brushed my sick thinking aside and said that the alcoholic must first put away the drink, then work the program in sobriety. I completed a lengthy residential program for recovery from addiction. When I got out, I continued to go to meetings, got a sponsor, and worked the Steps.

All of this time, however, my sexaholism was progressing. I was still masturbating, and I always had my eye out for harder forms of pornography. Sexual relations with my partner weren't right. I would leave it to her to initiate sex, and usually I would resort to fantasies during sex to feel satisfied. Talk of marriage made me uncomfortable. Without alcohol, I had more time to myself. I used to watch a woman in a house across the street, waiting for a glimpse of nudity. This was a form of acting out I hadn't engaged in when I was drinking.

One evening at an open AA meeting a man beside me introduced himself as a sexaholic. Next I heard that a group that called themselves Sexaholics Anonymous met on the premises; this was reportedly a program to deal with sexual addiction based on the principles of AA. I was taken aback when I tried to go to one of their meetings, only to be told that their meetings were closed. Would I like to come to an information meeting? At the information meeting two SA members told their stories briefly, but I found it hard to identify with either. During the weeks that followed, however, I thought a lot about my sexual behaviors. My Fourth and Fifth Steps were replete with sexual escapades I would rather forget. That was in the past, I told myself. I still went to "men's magazines" for escape, but didn't figure I needed a program to stop. As for masturbation, that was just a physical outlet that relieved tension. I was still practicing denial.

I read SA's Twenty Questions. Then I turned to the back of the brochure to see how I'd scored and what that meant. It appears I was still looking for a way out while looking for a way in. There were questions in the brochure that gave me pause, however. Did I still resort to masturbation, even though I was having all the sex I wanted? Did I still resort to images in my mind during sex? Did I want to get away from my partner quickly after having sex? What got my attention more than the fact that I would have to answer these questions affirmatively was that they were asked at all. Only a group that was dealing honestly with the answers would be asking these questions in the first place.

The "convincer" came to me from an SA member who told me that the key to the thing was lust. For him, he said, it started with sexual fantasies which affected his metabolism. Lust acted like a narcotic in his bloodstream. Once under the influence of lust, he acted out. This hit me. I could easily relate to this. I could be intoxicated on lust without acting out. It would only be a question of time before I needed stronger forms of lust. The bottom line was, I couldn't lust safely. Even if things didn't get any worse, lust was already making my life unmanageable. I was struck by the fact that this fellowship had identified the "first drink" and declared its powerlessness over that. Deep down something told me I had known it all along.

In some ways, it was a bitter pill to swallow. But admitting it promised freedom, too, just as admitting powerlessness over alcohol freed me from the compulsion to drink. As soon as I could admit I was a sexaholic, I was free not to act out. I found a line in *Sexaholics Anonymous* that summed up the First Step experience perfectly for me: "We were free to see and admit what we really were inside because we were finally free from having to act out what we were" (84). Immediately I saw the need to quit masturbating and give up all forms of media that could trigger my addiction. Since I wasn't married, it meant giving up sex with my partner. I also threw out phone numbers and addresses of women I'd met at meetings and in other fellowships.

I got an SA sponsor and started working the Steps anew, this time with the focus on sex, lust, and dependency. I called my sponsor and others every day, and we got current with temptations. Usually my sponsor would suggest we pray, as his sponsor had prayed with him. This felt uncomfortable in the beginning, just as ending meetings with a prayer had felt uncomfortable, but the benefits to my serenity were immediate.

After three months of sexual sobriety, I experienced a benefit not mentioned in the program. I quit smoking. I figured I couldn't feel any worse than I did without pornography, so I might as well quit this one, too. And for the first time I was able to let go of an addiction that had dogged me for twenty-five years.

I date my sexual sobriety to 1987, two years after I came into SA. I worked the program a day at a time, setting myself priorities I could handle. Getting to SA meetings, wherever available, took preference over everything else. My partner and I discovered we really didn't miss sex. I was free to be honest with her and not manipulate her for sex or other favors. After two years of recovery, we married. In marriage, we continued to use abstinence as a tool. Sex was optional now, but we found we needed recovery as a couple in order to be able to have sex. This took progressive willingness to be honest with each other, and time. I missed masturbation at times, but I had the fellowship of sobriety.

I started to enjoy life in a deeper way, made possible by a new and more honest relationship with God. The recovery I had in SA was deeper than the one I had experienced previously. Even though I experienced the "spiritual shock" of lust recovery spoken of in *Recovery Continues* (28 – 29), I wouldn't trade it for what I had before. I knew I was finally on the right path. I don't believe I'll ever get to the place where I'm no longer tempted to lust, but the temptation has never been stronger than it was at the beginning. When it seems to be stronger, that is because I haven't surrendered.

SA, more than any other, is a program of repetition. If I keep coming to meetings, working the Steps, and surrendering my will, I experience change. "What used to be the hunch or the occasional inspiration gradually becomes a working part of the mind," the AA Big Book tells us (87). I'm amazed that this is increasingly true for me. I'm grateful for the intimacy I have with my wife today. I'm grateful for the growing ability to be honest with others.

20. Glimpses of Sanity

Sobriety came one day in 1985 like an unexpected gift. Three weeks earlier I had learned that there were people who called themselves sex addicts and who held Twelve Step meetings. I had begun making a weekly 200-mile round trip to the closest meeting, a meeting that was unaffiliated with any national fellowship. I wanted sobriety, but this meeting didn't have a group definition of sobriety. They preferred to talk about bottom lines.

What was my bottom line? I kept questioning the other addicts, and I prayed that God would reveal His will for me. But deep inside myself, I already knew the answer. I knew that sexual fantasy made me drunk and that sobriety for me required abstinence from sexual fantasy. To be sober I would need to let go of the fantasy hits one at a time as they came. But my intellect saw that as a prescription for failure. I had struggled for years in prayer and anguish to break away from my fantasy life, and I had always failed. I was addicted to fantasy. It was mainly with fantasy that I administered the drug to myself. To pick up a white chip and declare to those other addicts that I was going to give up fantasy was to embrace failure.

As I prayed for God's will and the courage to carry it out, I experienced four days of freedom from sexual impulses such as I had never believed possible. Four days of serenity and clarity of mind. I took it as a sign from my Higher Power that I should go ahead and pick up that chip. It gave me the courage to embrace failure, to embrace powerlessness. I picked up the chip, and since that day I have surrendered the fantasy hits one at a time. Instead of failure, God gave me the gift of sobriety.

Looking back, I see more than ever what a free and unexpected gift sobriety was. But I also see my recovery as a continuum. At the time, sobriety seemed to come like a bolt from the blue, but now I see a Higher Power preparing me for ten years. For ten years, intermittently, I had been experiencing glimpses of sanity.

In other words, without knowing it, I was experiencing Step Two. Healing and gradual release from the insanity of addictive thinking began before sobriety and, thank God, have continued until today.

The early path to sanity for me was through Alcoholics Anonymous—and I'm not even an alcoholic! Ten years earlier, in 1975, I discovered that I qualified as an Al-Anon and began going to meetings. But I soon found myself attracted to open AA meetings. I certainly needed Al-Anon, but I felt more at home at AA meetings than anywhere else in the world. I didn't know why, but I kept going back. My recall of those days is not so sharp, but I would guess that I attended three or four meetings a week, maybe one Al-Anon and the rest open-discussion AA. I didn't take a sponsor (how, I asked myself, could I tell an Al-Anon sponsor that I lived in a fantasy world, masturbated compulsively, and had molested children?), and I didn't work the Steps at first. I just showed up again and again for five years. I soaked in the attention and the sense of self-worth that I got from the alcoholics and the Al-Anons, and I soaked in the sense of honesty around the tables. Emotional and literal honesty was something I had very little experience with because, in my mind, the truth about me was too terrible.

During those first five years, from 1975 to 1980, I saw lots of alcoholics walk in the door. Those who kept coming back and got sober became beautiful. That's the only way I can describe it. I saw it again and again, men and women, young and old, becoming beautiful. That made an impression on me. I didn't know what it meant to be beautiful, but I wanted it for myself.

Toward the end of that period I began seriously to explore how the Steps might apply in my life. Still without a sponsor, I stumbled through the first three Steps. I tried to open up and talk about myself at meetings. I can't say that I talked about my feelings because, drunk with lust, I didn't know much about feelings. But I began to open up. And the experience of others that I had been hearing around those tables began to make sense to me. I began to understand what they meant by gratitude, acceptance, prayer—not praying for what I want, but praying for God's will for me.

The year 1980 was a jumble of events. My first marriage came to an end. I acted out more extensively and more dangerously than ever before; at one point, I thought—mistakenly—that I had been caught at it, and the fear I experienced was enough to break through my denial and convince me that I was insane and out of control—a bottom for me, a First Step experience. I also had what I call a Second Step experience. I wrote out a Fourth Step, which mostly recorded my history of obsession and molesting. I gave my Fifth Step to a member of the clergy. Very brief moments of being "in the present" began to occur; I would be walking a corridor at work or sharpening a pencil, and then unbidden and only for a few seconds, I would actually know where I was. What a jumble that year was! I was drunk with obsession much of the time, and I don't have a clear memory of what happened when.

But I do remember something of how I experienced a new understanding of the Second Step and what it meant in my life. I was sitting in an AA open-discussion meeting that I had attended religiously for four years; I don't remember the topic. It came to me—I didn't know from where—that all my life I had felt responsible for knowing how events around me were supposed to work out and even for making things happen that way. I was supposed to figure it all out. Sometime early in life I had put myself in the place of God. I had been to enough meetings by that time to understand the absurdity of my thinking. In a flash, I saw that I had a choice between, on the one hand, continuing to take responsibility for making things turn out right—through manipulation and my own personal anguish—or, on the other hand, letting go and letting God—acknowledging that there is a Power greater than myself.

"Came to believe that a Power greater than ourselves . . ."—that part of Step Two was now more than a collection of words to me. It was a promise of release from a life of burden and misery. I was not sober, and I was numb much of the time, but I had nevertheless been given a glimpse of sanity.

That was 1980. It was another five years before I was ready for the gift of sobriety. I don't see that as lost time, but as a time of preparation. After I hit bottom—realizing now that my sexual behavior was out of control—I was drawn to attend even more open

AA meetings than before. I began telling my story to others, one on one, because I knew that Bill W. had stayed sober before he met Dr. Bob by finding drunks to tell his story to. Not expecting to find anyone else like me, I sought out a few people that I thought I could trust to hear my story, mainly sober alcoholics and members of my church. I was learning to bring the inside out. One day at a time, I molested no more children.

But I was continuously drunk. Drinking with my eyes. Living in fantasy stories. Never going more than a day and a half without masturbating. Yes, I tried again and again to stop masturbating, and when I occasionally made it to thirty-six hours I would feel heroic, as if I had set an Olympic record. But then I would masturbate four or five times in the next eight hours to celebrate. This had been the pattern of my life since adolescence. I was a sick man, and I had no name for my sickness but *perversion*.

Yet God was preparing me. I remember (and this is clearer in my memory) a weekly prayer meeting that a friend and I had at his service station, a two-man prayer meeting. I was learning to bring the inside out. I had told my story to this friend, and we shared our spiritual journeys week by week. I remember telling him more times than once that my craziness always started in my head with a fantasy. Nobody taught me that, and I didn't figure it out; it was an understanding that came to me from somewhere else, sick as I was. It was a glimpse of sanity.

So when I found that meeting of sex addicts in 1985, after ten years attending AA and Al-Anon meetings, I was willing to pick up a white chip and let go of the fantasy starts one day, one hour, one minute at a time. I didn't get sober in four days or in three weeks. For me, the gift of sobriety was a miracle, alright, but it was a miracle of the educational variety. For ten years God was preparing me so that, by the time I learned that the name for me was "sex addict," I was ready for the gift of sobriety.

The man who told me about that meeting of sex addicts one-hundred miles away also loaned me a copy of the SA manual. There was no SA in the state, so he and I started a meeting close to home. I got an SA sponsor.

Early in our relationship, he challenged me on my addict's habits of mind, especially what he called my intellectualizing. I wanted to figure things out. I wanted to know what was driving me to do the things I did, what was driving others to do the things they did, what I should do to make things come out right. My sponsor pointed out that my best thinking had only got me misery and insanity. Why didn't I get out of my head and just wait and see what God would do with my life? His words reminded me of my Second Step experience, in which the same truth that my sponsor was telling me had simply come to me out of nowhere, in the middle of an AA discussion meeting years earlier. And *that* reminded me that my intuition that sexual fantasy was what made me drunk had also come to me unbidden. Those were truths I had not figured out in my head. Now I began to believe that they came from God. And those brief experiences of being in the moment? They came from God too. Those too were glimpses of sanity.

Now I'm beautiful! That's right, beautiful—not perfect, but worthy of God's love and of the love of others. And I am able to love others, not perfectly, but more unselfishly than I thought possible. I used to think I was incapable of love. When I surrender my will to God's, I can be a blessing to others.

Early in sobriety, God removed from me the compulsion to masturbate. Over the years, I have experienced progressive freedom from the desire to build those fantasy stories that used to make me drunk. I have days or weeks at a time of freedom. But I know what to do if I'm not willing to surrender a sexual impulse immediately. I call another addict and admit my powerlessness. The action of making the call opens the door to surrender. One of my Higher Power's gifts to me is a continuing awareness of my First Step powerlessness.

I work the Steps actively with pen and paper. I perform service for the fellowship. I sponsor other sexaholics, including those in prison for sex offences; God has kept me in humble awareness that I could be in prison myself this very day. In my service work, I am learning to limit my commitments to those I can fulfill without putting unhealthy stress on me or on my family life.

I am learning how to live life on life's terms. I continue to experience periods of fear and of powerlessness over my ego, but I no longer keep these feelings a secret or try to figure out what to do about them by myself. I bring them out into the light with others as a way of turning them over to God.

My wife can tell you that I'm sometimes not an easy person to live with, but we have a good marriage. She works her S-Anon program and I work my SA program. We don't try to sponsor each other, but we do share our hopes and fears. I'm able to listen to her pretty well without trying to fix her (well, not *too* often, anyway). When I'm not capable of listening, I tell her that. God gives us both the patience to work through the daily give-and-take of child rearing, job pressures, and our individual bumps and rough spots.

I have more patience with myself as well. One day at a time, I accept my powerlessness. One day at a time, I practice gratitude for the healing and the sanity God has given me. Giving up my former role as the Higher Power has been a very slow process, but my sponsor—and my own experience—have convinced me that my own thinking never got me to the truth. The truth comes as a gift from a Power greater than myself.

Some years ago, my sponsor told me, "When it's time for you to start thinking, I'll let you know." He hasn't given me the go-ahead yet, and today I'm not in a hurry.

21. True Intimacy

For more than forty years, I thought that intimacy and sexual activity were the same thing. I also thought of myself as a homosexual, entitled to secretly engage in sex with other males whenever I felt the need or desire to do so. The burden of leading a double life brought me to the point of misery and despair. I may have been gay, but I certainly wasn't happy.

At age fifty-four, just a few weeks after a brush with mortality, I opened the phone book and found a telephone number for Sexaholics Anonymous. From my very first meeting, I knew I was home.

Today I am very grateful to SA, to the Twelve Steps and to the God of my understanding for a wonderful new life. As a result of surrendering lust one day at a time, I am now able to experience true intimacy with men, women and children, with myself and with my God. It's such a healthy feeling for me to be in the presence of a handsome young man and not to be triggered by lust. I can now relate to that person, not as a face or other physical feature, but as another human being.

From the time I was a child, I suffered from body envy. I never felt on the inside like other guys looked on the outside. That led to years of organizing my life around such false perceptions. I don't have to do that today. Through recovery in SA, I have learned how to relate to men as whole persons. I don't have to reduce them to objects of lust or fantasize having a romance with them. Because I choose to use the tools of recovery in SA, I do not have to keep lust churning around inside my head. I can call my sponsor or another member of the program and give it away to them. That is a wonderful gift of this program.

It has been eleven years since I shared my First Step inventory of powerlessness and unmanageability. I sat in a SA meeting full of men, and disclosed to them my countless sexual escapades with other men. Surely they would think of me as a hopeless pervert, or so I feared. Yet when I finished giving away my First Step, all they said was "Thanks." Then, one by one, they thanked me for my courage and honesty and for reminding them of their own feelings of shame and guilt. That was the day I really learned the meaning of the Twelve Step saying, "We're only as sick as our secrets."

When I look back on my forty-five years of addiction to lust, I remember how I struggled to come to terms with the issue of sexual orientation. Although I never felt comfortable openly identifying myself as gay, I did hang out with a lot of people who were openly gay. Yet I also remember as a young man having girlfriends, wanting to do sexual things with them, and competing with other guys for their affection.

I always framed my problems in terms of being straight or gay, but in recovery, I have learned that I can put this issue completely behind me. Thanks to the spiritual awakening I have experienced as the result of working the Twelve Steps of SA recovery, I now realize that I'm not gay . . . I'm not straight . . . I'm just an unconditionally loved and forgiven child of God, a struggling, growing, good human being who happens to have a history of acting out sexually with males.

I used to define myself by my sexual feelings and desires, but today I no longer do that. I have a personal history that is so much richer than my sexual feelings and desires. Today, I still experience some same-sex attraction, but I don't have to act on it. I owe all of this to my discovery of the SA solution. Our literature says our solution is not for everyone, but it certainly works for me and for countless others like me.

As it turns out, I really did have a problem with orientation. I once oriented my life around myself and around my sexual desires for men. Today, I orient my life around God, as I understand Him. It is He who has given me the gifts of sexual sobriety, sanity, and serenity. By God's grace I am happy, joyous, and free. That's more than enough for me.

22. Yet Strangely Content

I am a British sexaholic. I was forty-two years old when I first heard the phrase "sex addiction." I had just been through the catastrophic collapse of a second marriage and a second career. In response to these events I had fled to a New Age community in Scotland and was just about to dive headlong into a third career and a third marriage. The impact on me of those two words, sex addiction, was staggering. My mind went into a spin. I had difficulty standing upright. I couldn't have walked in a straight line.

I had just been comprehensively Twelfth-Stepped by a couple who were visiting from London. They shared their experience of being sex and relationship addicts and introduced me to a novel concept—sexual sobriety. I identified and made the commitment to four self-defined "bottom lines"—no pornography, no masturbation, no sex outside a committed relationship, and no relationship for the foreseeable future. We started a meeting in Scotland. I began Step work, went to just about any meeting I could find in any fellowship, got a sponsor from AA, uncovered some experiences of childhood sexual abuse, spent six weeks in treatment in the United States, and did loads and loads of therapy. For four years, by the grace of God, I was sober.

By the end of my fourth year of sobriety, I had become something of a Twelve Step fellowship guru. I knew everything there was to know about my ways of acting out and why I had become a sex addict. My recovery model was, "Find out who you are and be that person." I spent a lot of time in therapy but, incidentally, found very little of any real worth. I parted company with my first sponsor and got myself ready for a relapse.

The addiction is cunning, so it easily found the chink in my spiritual armour. I came to the conclusion that after four years of sobriety, it was time to let go of my fourth bottom line—no relationship for the foreseeable future. Soon I was in the grip of an addictive relationship with a violent partner and powerless to stop.

After several failed attempts to set and maintain the necessary boundaries, I had an unwelcome insight. I began to suspect that either I would have to change my sobriety definition to "no sex outside marriage," or I would remain in the clutches of my addiction. I didn't want to make the change, so I held out against this horrendous idea for another week. Finally I surrendered and made the commitment. The impact was immediate. I stepped onto good spiritual ground. I was able to set effective boundaries with my partner, end my acting out, and withdraw from the relationship with sobriety and serenity.

I moved from Scotland back to England eleven days later and rented a flat about five miles from where my three children were living with their mother and her new partner. It was surely no coincidence that two months later I met a man who told me he belonged to a fellowship called Sexaholics Anonymous, which employed a sobriety definition very like my new one. I went to an SA convention and got an SA sponsor. My new sponsor was very impressed with my experience of Twelve Step recovery. I used him as an unpaid therapist, but I did not get well. I stayed sober, but my physical and spiritual condition began to decline markedly. I began losing weight quite rapidly. This was when I hit bottom.

After I had shared my arrogant and rebellious mind at a second SA convention, a long-sober SA member confronted me with the fact that I was "on a different track." I felt this like a punch in the stomach. On the train home that day, I felt angry, lonely, and confused. If I accepted that I was on the wrong track, then I had to either follow it to the end, or get off it and get onto the SA track. After another struggle I decided to really join the fellowship. A lot of things changed in a very short time. I began to recover my lost weight. I fired my sponsor/therapist and asked my confronter to sponsor me. I rejoined the religion that I had abandoned twenty-five years earlier. I came off sickness benefit and got my first job after six years of unemployment. Finally, a major change occurred in my thinking and attitudes, especially as they related to my former wife and our family.

As each one of these changes was very profound I will unpack them a little before moving on.

The complete surrender of my right to eat the way I wanted seems to have been the key to my recovery around food. In the same way, complete surrender of my right to sexual activity on my own terms seems to have brought recovery in that area of my life.

My new sponsor helped me to understand that his job was not to listen to my harrowing but beautifully delivered tales. His job was to share his experience, strength, and hope with me as a fellow traveller with more sobriety. My job was to listen and to try taking the actions that he took to see if they worked for me too. His way was not, "Find out who you are and be that person," but "Who I am is none of my business. I'm just here to serve." I tried his way and it worked much better than mine. I came to see that all my knowledge about sex addiction, and why I had become an addict, was actually unimportant. All I needed to know was that there is a proven reliable method by which I can arrest my addiction. Once I knew that, all I had to do was take the necessary actions, and recovery was assured for me.

Rejoining the church was perhaps the biggest surrender of all. It was certainly my biggest fear. Such fears are the beacon light of my growth. The journey was a long one. For twenty-five years I had sampled a variety of spiritual modes. My final bridge back was a meditation group. For a while I thought I could hold it there. I could sit in meditation every Sunday and think of myself as "almost religious." However, I did perhaps my most profound Fourth Step specifically about my relationships with religion. When this was complete, I took the Fifth Step with the local minister. This was like shifting the accumulated debris of a lifetime. Finally, after a retreat at which I found my mind completely fed but my heart dying of thirst, I made another of those now familiar surrenders. I decided to go to the church, park my brain at the door, and go in. I stood when they stood, kneeled when they kneeled, sang when they sang, and let God be God. I've never missed a service since. When you are home you know it.

When I had abandoned my wife and children, I had had no difficulty in blaming the whole business on my wife. She had insisted that she did not want to have sex with me, so that was the end of that! In my struggle with the "no sex outside marriage" issue, I had finally seen the depth of my faithlessness and the bankruptcy of my ideas about commitment. Today, the only true commitment is lifelong marriage—and that commitment does not end just because one partner says no to sexual activity. Repeated inventory work showed me how my wife and children had borne the brunt of my addiction and that amends were due in full measure. Once again surrender was required as I came to realize that full measure meant rebuilding the family that I had earlier broken. It has not happened yet and may never happen. Through this particular wound, I am being taught patience, forgiveness, constancy, and faithfulness—virtues so sadly lacking in this particular sexaholic.

For my first five years in recovery I did not have a regular job. I worked part time in a spiritual community, cleaning floors and lavatories. This gave me time to do my Step work, therapy appointments, meetings, and treatment. Initially I received a pension from my former business. When that ceased, I was classified as sick and began receiving sickness benefits. This had a slowly corrosive effect on me. By the time I had found SA, I considered myself unemployable and unlikely ever to work again. My occasional visits to the doctor were mainly about proving that I was still unfit for work so that I could continue to receive benefits. This attitude of helplessness and hopelessness undoubtedly contributed to my low bottom. Surrender came when I called a sober member of the fellowship who had recently been helped out of a similar hole and asked him to sponsor me back into work. Within two weeks, I had a job. This allowed me to build up my fitness for work and to develop the resilience which I had lost during my time off. In the next three years I had three other jobs before finding myself in a well-paid job specializing in e-commerce.

I have been sober in AA since 1991 and in SA since 1995. I am abstinent around food, employed, a member in good standing of my local church, and faithfully holding my family in love. Considering where I have come from, this is a miracle due entirely to the grace of God. All I have done is work a program of recovery to the best of my ability.

What does this look like in practice?

Meetings, lots of meetings. For the first few years I averaged five meetings a week in different fellowships. I now live in an area where there are lots of Twelve Step meetings and usually do two SA meetings a week. I prefer meetings that study fellowship literature, the Steps, and the Traditions. These really do help me to maintain a fitter spiritual condition.

I have an *SA sponsor* whom I phone every week. I try very hard to tell him the things I would rather keep secret and act on his suggestions no matter what.

Working the Steps. This is the fourth time through for me.

Starting new meetings is something I have done on several occasions. There was a time when I could not find another sexaholic, so I just started a meeting anyway. My dog and I kept that meeting going for about two years. During that time we had just three visitors, including one from Ireland and one from Germany.

Service has helped me to stay sober. I have held a number of different service positions at group and intergroup levels. I have experienced the shift from reluctant to glad server. It took some time, but I just needed to practice harder! I used to believe that I was unsuccessful at these jobs because I did not do them well. Now I remind myself that I am brilliantly successful because I have stayed sober.

I have *sponsored sexaholics*. It does not always keep them sober, but it certainly helps me. If I have not heard from a sponsee for three days, I consider myself fired. I'm always delighted to hear from a lost sponsee again, but I want to know what will be different this time.

I go to any *conventions* that are held in the UK and have also been to one in the US and several in Ireland. At first, I disliked them and felt very self-conscious and uncomfortable. Nowadays I really look forward to being with my SA buddies.

Making amends. My experience in making amends has been patchy. Things went poorly whenever I had a hidden agenda or when I was temporarily without a sponsor and going it alone. On other occasions I have been able to make full amends, bring healing into the lives of others, and drop a huge burden of guilt.

Abstinence. The unfashionable virtue of chastity has become a real treasure in my life. I am sober just one day at a time, but I want a chaste life every day from now on.

Prayer. I have a prayer life today. I am beginning to discern the extraordinary workings of a loving and merciful God and how He has shaped and ordered the life of one sexaholic.

Gratitude. I believe that it is God's grace that really keeps me sober. I have seen others do as much if not more than I and still relapse. Somehow God's grace is reaching me. This is a miracle and a mystery.

The rest of my life is up to God. My life has certainly not turned out the way I imagined it would; yet I am strangely content with what it is. Therein is a miracle.

23. The Hope of a Program That Works

It is difficult for me to think back over my life before I discovered Sexaholics Anonymous. It is difficult to express my gratitude to SA for the positive gift of life I have received. I believe I can begin to express it by sharing some of my story. I was a lonely, rebellious four-year-old farm boy when I began disrobing in secret and finding pleasure in women's pictures in the family medical book. At seven I discovered delirious pleasure climbing ropes and trees. My mother's angry reaction to my self-stimulation and my fear of my father's violence drove me to secrecy. Masturbation was soon a full-blown obsession. A priest insisted I would go to hell for masturbating, but I could not stop. I felt God would never love or forgive me until I could remain sexually "pure." My sexual addiction locked love and God out of my life before I was ten, beginning a long life of separation from God—hell on Earth.

When I was ten, we three brothers and my parents moved closer to town and nearer to neighbors with girls. By then I was acting out with objects and simulating the sex act alone. I watched farm animals, and I sexually abused pets. The neighborhood mothers' committee banned me from visiting any family with girls as a result of my "king on the mountain" behavior with girls. A missionary book with explicit pictures brought greater arousal. Now my imagination turned ordinary writing and pictures into personal pornography. Spying a neighbor girl preparing for bed initiated nightly peeping and a lifelong career of voyeurism and cruising. Cross-dressing, fetishism with women's clothing, a breast fixation—all became rituals accompanying masturbation. My brother and I had to sleep together, and I abused him while he slept. Believing one was not responsible for dreams led me to efforts to have sexual dreams. Acting out in sleep followed, with increasing fear of detection.

By my mid-teens I was so aroused in mixed company that I feared orgasm without contact, yet I "accidentally" touched girls on student trips and was horribly ashamed when confronted. In junior high school I was convinced that I was a "sex fiend," terrified that compulsive sex would lead to abuse and sex crimes. Fear-driven, I consciously gave up hope of exclusive relationships with girls or of ever marrying. High school drinking episodes increased my sexual drive, adding a new fear of alcoholism, which was rampant in my family.

At eighteen, I graduated from high school with honors and was hospitalized with tuberculosis in my foot. Five weeks in the hospital opened a new world of sexualized back rubs, exposing self, painting nudes as a hobby, peeking, and touching the nurses who cared for me. I believed that my sexual behavior prevented healing and that divine retribution caused my scholarship to M.I.T. to be cancelled. My mother arranged for me to live with my aunt and uncle in the city and drive a truck for my uncle. That arrangement ended abruptly and shamefully when I was caught peeping at my young cousin in her bath. Completely separated from family, I got into group voyeurism. Fears of homosexuality were awakened when I taught a teenager to masturbate.

At twenty I was "that foul-mouthed kid with wings on his truck," addicted to "bennies," barbiturates, and speed, and I was supporting my younger brothers, whom my mother had sent to spy on me. We enrolled in an all-male religious college. I worked fifty-five to sixty-five hours a week, maintained third place in my class, and still managed to binge sexually on weekends. The guilt and shame of living a double life was crushing. With little desire to live, I confided in a priest-teacher and laughed demonically when he suggested I change my life by becoming a priest. Two months later I entered the ten-year seminary training leading to the priesthood. On my twenty-first birthday I entered a prestigious seminary in the Midwest. That same night I got drunk on the wine reserved for use at Mass. The dormitory and observed living enabled me to achieve a few weeks of celibacy. However, a private room and popular magazine pictures triggered acting out again.

The next forty-five years never produced a single week of celibacy. I chose to be ordained without achieving the six months of celibacy which was a condition prior to life commitment. The second day after ordination I was drunk and acting out sexually. To my double-life misery I had now added a new hell of public hypocrisy and fear of embarrassing the Church and my religious community.

The next twenty years were spent in the Near East, where religious custom favored strict segregation of women. I appeared successful: teaching in college, helping the poor, running innovative literacy programs. At the same time I made a virtue of destroying my health, venting my hatred of my body. Although terrified of detection and the danger of expulsion or even death, I could not stop acting out or break the daily ritual of daylight hours spent peeping through opera glasses into the women's walled compounds below. Night was pornography and fantasy time, and also make-up time working to the wee hours, compensating for wasted daytime work hours. The "sacrifice" brought a hated reputation for devotion. Vacation periods were spent sexualizing among the tribal people in volunteer work. Stateside leaves for therapy and study failed to bring relief. I covered sexual activity by getting graduate degrees with honors. I returned to the East for four final years of frenetic activity. Moved by my continuous self-destruction, my religious brothers banished me permanently to the States. For many weeks, I had been concealing active tuberculosis while I struggled to protect my uplift programs for the poor—thus threatening the health of the very people I served.

Bitter and humiliated, I reported to a religious recuperation center and burned with resentment for the "unchristian" treatment I had been subjected to by my religious brothers. I retaliated by entering my first relationship with a woman. Within weeks I had experienced the gamut of sex, short of marriage. Sexual activity and spiritual, intellectual, and emotional deterioration progressed together as my public career collapsed in ruin. I was terminated from numerous teaching positions, from parish assignments, and finally fired from volunteer jobs! This spelled an end to all church or education-related employment. With reality crowding in, I escaped into a mental hospital where fantasy and sexual acting out completely frustrated treatment. Humiliated but not humbled, I returned to my religious community diagnosed as a manic-depressive with some promise of normal living through continuous psychotherapy and mood-stabilizing medication.

Still resentful at the authorities for ending my career, I set out on unrestrained sexual binging in multiple relationships, adultery, incestuous entanglements, and complete surrender to rituals of masturbation. My religious superiors refused to kick me out of the priesthood, and I was afraid to try to make it outside on my own. Psychiatrists continued to offer therapy based on incorrect diagnoses. A job was created for me at an alcohol and drug treatment center for skid row disaffiliates. It takes a con to catch a con, and I was frightened of the clients, deservedly. After more than two years, the skid row alcoholics forced me to admit to alcohol and drug addiction and to start attending AA and NA as an "underground" member lest I lose my job. After two more years, I was clean, sober, and miserable. Reading the poem "Footprints" for the first time, I screamed in rage and despair, "God, stop carrying me deeper and deeper into hell and let me die." I had stopped acting out with others, but simply gave in to the masturbation rituals.

After another year of depressed alcohol and drug sobriety, I received the SA brochure from an anonymous counselor. My first reading of "The Problem," "The Solution," and "Test Yourself" (the Twenty Questions) turned on the light: "I am powerless over lust and sex *because I am addicted*." From my first SA meeting, I was home with members who understood me, and who demonstrated hope and the shared miracle of recovery. Surrender triggered withdrawal pangs much greater than alcohol and drug withdrawal. But I had *the hope of a program that works!* For the first time, I was not alienated from God and felt I was accepted and loved. Progress through the Steps was not smooth or painless. Old practices and playmates led to two relapses. Another relapse followed from striving for too-rapid progress and instant perfection. Progressively I have surrendered gambling, workaholism, all stimulants, and playing God in other people's recovery. Currently I am surrendering TV and popular reading because of my deep-rooted tendency to sexualize programs and publications. Tears still come with awareness of the pain, suffering, and worry my behavior and failure brought to my blood and religious family members. I am hypercritical of self and others. My efforts to carry the message are not always successful for others, but they have kept me sober, one day at a time, since 1986. My image of God as loving and forgiving is slowly healing the pain and blame of a dysfunctional childhood and a wasted religious life. Through the practice of prayer and meditation, I am coming to experience peace and serenity.

24. It Keeps Getting Better

I can hear my sponsor's voice, passing on the words from his sponsor and his sponsor's sponsor: "Things get worse; IT gets better." I do not have to wonder any more what IT is. For me today, IT means life, serenity, acceptance, gratitude, living without expectations, finding the power to be useful, and carrying out God's will for me. When I came to Sexaholics Anonymous in 1988, I had none of IT. Things were getting pretty bad in my life, family, and work; however, I was getting ready for a change.

I learned about Sexaholics Anonymous when a counselor, during an emergency session with my wife and me, reacted to my explanation of my repeated adulterous affairs. "I guess I just need to be involved with more than one woman at a time," I said to her. She replied, "You're a sex addict!" My first SA miracle occurred at that moment. I looked at her and said, "You're right." I felt goose bumps that day in August. I had been called by my true name for the first time. I am a sex addict. I knew when she said it that I had been a sex addict for over thirty-five years. Finally, someone saw me for who I truly was. I felt great relief.

She gave me a phone number. I called it, and within two hours I spoke with my first official SA contact. Two hours after that I met him at my first SA meeting on a Tuesday night. Twenty-four hours earlier I had been sitting paralyzed with fear in our living room as my wife confronted me about having lunch with a lust partner and told me I'd have to move out. She was emotionally dissolving in front of me. All I could do was sit frozen and wonder how I'd get out of it this time. Why did I torture this woman I loved so much?

At my first meeting, I learned some important facts. There would be people in this anonymous program who knew me. One man there that first night was a fellow professional whose arrest had been reported on the front pages of the local newspaper. My compulsive masturbation, sexual fantasies, voyeurism, use of pornography, multiple affairs, and exhibitionism were shared with others. Feeling so awful and guilty and helpless about these behaviors was normal for a sexaholic. I also learned that there is an answer to the question I had asked myself twenty-two years and two marriages earlier. Could I ever look at a woman and not imagine being sexual with her, no matter who she was, or how old she was, or what she was doing? They told me that night that if I kept coming back and if I worked these Twelve Steps, eventually sex could really be optional for me.

In the next few weeks and months, I began to see that I was a sex drunk. While I had no history of alcohol or drug addiction, I got as intoxicated on lust and lust images as any alcoholic gets on booze. Pornography, sadomasochism, bondage games, cross-dressing, romantic and sexual pursuits of women, attempting to seduce a teenager, touching a girl inappropriately, multiple adulterous affairs, and sexualizing every person and situation I encountered every day were each and all part of my drinking pattern. I was the kind of sex drunk who never lets the glass—or fantasy images—run dry. I was always sipping on lust in some shape or form. I realized that for over thirty years I had not been sober for even one day. My acting out was getting worse and increasingly dangerous both to myself and to others.

For quite a while things got better. Though I came into SA an atheist, I acted as if I could pray, surrender to a Higher Power, and ask for temptations and lust to be removed. If I could not use the words "God" or "Lord," I would say, "Master" (which I thought of in the sense of a teacher); I could think of my Higher Power as the collective wisdom of humanity. Eventually, pretty much as it says in the AA literature, I came to believe that "God" was a good description for a Higher Power. I found that the question of whether or not there is a God only distracted me from my need to surrender lust. I was willing to surrender to God, as I understood him. That worked for me.

My marriage slowly came back toward health. My wife was active in S-Anon and sought the help she needed to deal with her anger toward me, toward the other women, and toward those who had enabled my disease. After about eighteen months, I realized that I had stopped mentally ending our marriage. I had done this every day for the first twelve years of our marriage. I made the commitment that, no matter what, I am married to my wife and that's what God wants for me. My job is to carry my weight and responsibility in the marriage. Any thoughts of another marriage or relationship are fantasies—and toxic ones at that.

My children seemed to appreciate that I was home more often. Though it took several years, the rage attacks on them (and the dogs) gradually lessened. My work life seemed to steadily improve as I became less obsessed with being everywhere and doing everything. Much of what I had done at work before was trying either to lessen my guilt or to set up lusting situations with women.

As I listened in meetings, I learned that the social nudity at home as I was growing up was abusive for me. Eventually after several years, I had to forgive my parents and to repent having desired that they be different from the way they actually were. I learned that they and I were always doing the best we could do at the time. Sometimes my "best" was destructive, and other times it was helpful.

I did not know that it takes years for these things to change, nor did I know how many costs and consequences there might be along the way. "Things get worse; IT gets better." After four and a half years of sobriety, I was very comfortable with my progress in recovery. God decided that I needed more humility, that I needed an opportunity "to match calamity with serenity," as the Big Book says. I chose to share the basics of my addiction and recovery with my employers in a somewhat public meeting. I believed most people would accept me for the changed person I was. While most did accept my recovery, some could not. This led to the loss of my employment and profession after thirteen years in that city.

With the help of my sponsor, I moved into a new profession. I worked for about a year in two different states. In the second job I shared with my unit director the nature of my addiction and recovery (after he asked). He fired me immediately. I was really shaken and depressed for the next two years.

My wife told me I had to work, so I applied to a temporary employment agency. The temp work included stuffing envelopes, being a receptionist, and working as the office manager and secretary of a law firm for a year. I found this humiliating and freeing at the same time. At the end of that year, God found a new use for me in a helping profession, which I worked at for the next three years. During this time I learned some of the most important life lessons I have learned in sobriety.

I learned to reduce my expectations for income. I learned to respect my anonymity as a recovering sexaholic; not having done this before had cost me two jobs. I learned that I had grown up crippled in my ways of handling emotions. With the help of a therapist, I did some major growing up as well as accepting my character defects at a deeper level. I also learned (over and over again) that whatever I think I cannot give up in my life is exactly what I must surrender if I want to keep growing in recovery. Through God's grace, I have been willing to do that so far.

Much has happened in the past two years. I have been diagnosed with cancer and gone through surgery and radiation therapy. My sponsor was essential in keeping my focus on God and on willingness to value each moment of life that He gives me. I can feel my values shifting as I view mortality. I am aware now what wonderful gifts God gives me to share with others on a daily basis.

I have twice experienced the need to change sponsors for different reasons. Having a person who knows me through and through, who can recognize how I am doing just from the tone of my voice, is one of this program's greatest gifts.

I have been restored to my former profession. Thanks to my wife's urging, I do so on a part-time basis. Since I learned that God truly will provide as much money as we need, I am permitted to work reasonable hours and to have time to take care of my health, to do service work, and to pursue my avocations.

As my sponsors said, while things may get worse, or better, or just stay the same for a while, IT keeps getting better! For the grace, serenity, and joy of sobriety, and for the opportunity to grow as God wants me to grow, rather than as my ego and fantasies were leading me for all those years, I can never be sufficiently grateful.

25. Half Measures

All my life, all I wanted was to fit in, to be accepted, and to feel okay about myself. I grew up in a family where there were multiple addictions. I was a loner. From very early on I hated myself. I felt trapped, always wishing and waiting to grow up so I could do what I wanted and have the freedom to get away from it all.

I found in fantasy a way to escape from the pain, fear, and sadness that were so much of my early life. Fantasy began with daydreaming about how I was a superhero and could bring justice to all. I would fantasize about being praised for all the good things I did and for saving the world. Only in fantasy did I feel alive, powerful, and good about myself. I hated having to return to reality.

One day, while in bed fantasizing, I began fondling myself and had an ejaculation. Not knowing anything about sex, I panicked. I thought I had somehow injured myself. I kept it to myself. The next day, I realized that I wasn't injured, and I remembered the good sensation I had felt. I returned to my bedroom and did it again. From this moment, I was hooked. I began looking for more and more opportunities to masturbate. It was all I thought about. Like fantasy, masturbation made me feel powerful. There seemed to be something magical about it.

I began showing how I could masturbate to my younger cousins and siblings. "Look what I can do!" I would feel special as they watched me and envied me. Soon I started walking down the street and exposing myself to others—still a youngster, yet feeling like a man! I knew I could get in trouble for such behavior, so I always kept far enough away not be recognized.

Once I was old enough to drive, I bought a used car and sought to get away, to have the freedom I always wanted. I still wanted desperately to fit in, so in spite of my childhood promises to myself to refrain from alcohol and other drugs, I began drinking alcohol and soon graduated to other drugs. I also began dealing drugs, and for the first time in my life I had what I called "friends." My parents couldn't believe how many phone calls I was getting. I felt special—I had friends.

I then discovered that getting high *and* masturbating was more thrilling than only having sex or only getting high. With this discovery, my addiction really took off. I began cruising and masturbating in my car. I would spend hours driving around, lusting after people and searching for the most attractive ones to masturbate to. I desperately wanted a sexual encounter with someone, anyone.

Soon I began to expose myself from my car. I would get high first. I was fearful about acting out this way, but under the influence I took many risks. Up to this point I didn't see anything wrong in my behavior. I was young and had a powerful sex drive, and I really didn't believe that I was hurting anybody.

In a couple of years I became obsessed with thoughts about sex with strangers. I did little dating because I feared rejection by women. I only dated women who made it clear that they were interested in me first. I could not keep a relationship for more than six months. I feared sex with the women I dated because I believed I would be rejected for not being muscular and macho.

While cruising one day, I picked up a male hitch-hiker and we got high together. One thing led to another and I propositioned him. He accepted, and I crossed into another level of my addiction. After this experience I felt ashamed and afraid, wondering what my friends would say if they found out what I did. I also questioned my sexuality. I was attracted to women, yet I found sex with men exciting as well. Rationalizing that nobody would know me there, I returned to the area where I had picked up this guy and discovered it was a cruising area for men. I began picking up men on a regular basis. I was now hooked on this new way of acting out—I couldn't stop.

My life and thinking were becoming more and more centered around sex: how many partners I could get, how often I could have sex, and how I could keep this life of mine secret. I began spending more and more time cruising, started building a pornography collection, and kept a written log of my sexual encounters. I would leave my house to go to a family function or a party and never make it there, in spite of having every intention of attending. More and more I was losing control over my behavior, and I couldn't stop.

Then I was arrested for indecent exposure. This was the first time. I couldn't believe this happened to me. I was so afraid, ashamed, and depressed. My parents bailed me out and found out about my secret life. I could hardly face them. However, they said little about it. The police blotter in the community newspaper included some minor details of my arrest, and I was devastated. This was it. No more acting out. I swore off all this behavior, began Twelve-Step meetings for my drug addiction, and really thought this was going to be the end of my sexual acting out. No way was I going to allow that to happen to me again.

Within a month I returned to acting out on the streets, rationalizing that as long as I avoided the area where I was arrested, I would be okay. About one year later I was arrested again. Once again I couldn't believe this had happened. I really wasn't a criminal. I wasn't violent. Why were they doing this to me? I was so far into my addiction that I could not see the wrong or the dangers of my behavior. I even tried to kill myself.

About two weeks later I was back on the streets again. I managed to avoid exposing myself and limited myself to picking up willing partners off the street. Herpes was becoming a big scare at that time, and it became harder to find partners. I became more desperate. I had sworn to myself that I would never pay for sex because that would mean something was really wrong if I needed it that badly. However, I began picking up prostitutes and paying for sex. Soon after descending to this new level of acting out, I was arrested for solicitation.

In the course of my addiction I was arrested seven or eight times. Each time, I promised myself and my family that this was it—no more!—only to return to it almost immediately. I also caught sexually transmitted diseases four times. Fortunately they were curable. Each time I swore I would stop acting out. What I failed to see was that I couldn't stop. On two separate occasions I even had a gun put to my head for approaching people whom I mistakenly thought were cruising. After talking myself out of being shot, I resumed soliciting a block away. That's how insane I had become. Despite being in Twelve-Step recovery for drug addiction, I had no idea that I could also be addicted to sex. I thought I had become the evil person my addicted parents said I would.

The judge ordered me to get counseling for my sexually dysfunctional behavior. My "expert" therapist proclaimed that I should find a nice girl and settle down, and then my sexual needs would be met in this relationship. This is what I really wanted. I continued to work with the therapist for the next three years. I found a nice girl in the Twelve-Step program I was attending, and we began a relationship. I thought I finally had the solution. I was feeling better about life, and my acting out diminished to masturbating with pornography at home.

I also entered seminary. I thought if I gave myself to God, the strong urge for sex would diminish. For a while everything seemed to be going well. I thought I had found the answer.

The girl I was dating lived about 45 minutes away from my house, and after several months it began taking me longer and longer to get home. I began to cruise again, at first only to look; before long I returned to all my old behaviors. This time the police came to the seminary to arrest me. The shame I felt was unbearable. I left the seminary. I lost the girl I was dating. My therapist didn't know what to do. I didn't know where to turn. Once again, I was suicidal.

During this same week, information on sex addiction was presented both on television and in the newspaper. I immediately sent for more information and read it. They were talking about me! I couldn't believe that there were others like me and that there was a place for help. I was used to reading about how there was no cure for sex offenders, and I had felt hopeless up to this point.

The information included readings from Sexaholics Anonymous. When I saw that SA uses the same Twelve Steps as the program I was going to for my drug addiction, I thought that maybe I really didn't need to go to SA, just modify my own program of recovery to include my sexual behavior. Actually, I was afraid to go to SA because I thought I might see someone I knew there— and what would they think?! Of course I never worried about who knew me at bookstores, parks, and jail.

I developed a homemade program of recovery. I got rid of all the pornography and all my drugs and stopped cruising for street partners. However, I really believed that I had to have sex in some form, so I limited myself to masturbation two or three times per week for no more than ten minutes at a time. I attended my Twelve Step meetings for drug addiction but was too ashamed to tell them about my sex addiction. For about three months I was able to keep to this plan. Then, one day while masturbating for my ten-minute limit, the urge for more grew so intense that I stopped what I was doing, dressed, and went cruising. In a couple of weeks I had returned to all my past sexual behaviors and to using drugs as well. I was arrested again. I finally came to see that my way was not working; I needed SA.

I was scared to death when I attended my first SA meeting. I didn't know what to expect. I listened, and when it was my turn to share, all I could do was cry. In fact, for the first six meetings I attended, I was in so much pain that I would break down and cry before my first sentence ended. I had thought I was the only one who acted out as I did; it was reassuring to hear that I was not alone. It took quite some time before I could name all the behaviors I engaged in because I was too ashamed to admit to them. But hearing others talk openly about their past and how they were achieving progressive victory over lust gave me real hope.

When I understood that the sobriety definition specified no sex with self or anyone but the spouse, I panicked. I didn't think this would be possible for me. Most of those attending SA meetings in my area were either older or married. I rationalized that either they were too old for sex or they were having sex regularly with their spouses, and that's why they could be sober. I became a chronic slipper. I knew I needed SA, yet I was still rebelling, still doing things my way, still thinking I would die if I didn't have some kind

116

of sex. I practiced "half measures": going to two or three meetings a week, making phone calls after a slip, not before, and sometimes reading program literature. I even prayed. Yet I didn't really want to give up my "best friend." I would engage in fantasy or objectify while driving. I would push myself so close to the limit that when I did slip I felt like a victim, believing that I really was not responsible for my acting out. It was too powerful; how could I be expected to resist it?

This pattern lasted for seven years. Sponsors fired me, and I was even arrested once while in the program. I was losing the hope I felt early in SA. Yet somehow I remembered what someone said at my first meeting: "Keep coming back." That was perhaps the only thing I did right during this time. I felt caught in the middle. I really didn't want to give up acting out all together, but I was afraid of what would happen to me if I left the program and returned to active addiction. So I would fool myself into thinking that at least I had made some progress in SA. So what if I slipped on occasion?

Then, I relapsed. I went on a several-day binge that included all my past behaviors, even substance abuse after having several years of drug sobriety. I didn't get arrested this time, but I woke up spiritually, physically, and emotionally exhausted. Once again I was suicidal. I couldn't even look at myself in the mirror. Several years in SA and I still couldn't get it right. I cannot begin to describe the utter pain and desperation I felt. I expected that soon I would end up in jail, in an institution, or dead. I wanted out of this insanity, and for the first time I was actually willing to do whatever I had to do to get better.

I got out the *Sexaholics Anonymous* text, read the section "How I Overcame My Obsession with Lust," and prayed for strength. I pondered what I needed to do to make the program my life, not just something to spend some time on between episodes of acting out. The time I had in the program helped at this point. I knew what to do; I had heard it said so many times before but never really understood—or maybe I really didn't want to understand. I needed to attend more meetings; two or three per week were not enough for me. I was attending a night course at college for work, and I really enjoyed it; but it was preventing me from attending more meetings. I went to school that night and dropped out. I cried all the way home. I now understood that I had a life-threatening condition and that if I didn't accept the limitations I need to have in my life, I wouldn't survive. While driving home and crying, I made my first prayer of surrender to God. I remembered the line from "How It Works," which says, "Rarely have we seen a person fail who has thoroughly followed our path" (*AA* 58). The word was *thoroughly*! No more doing the Twelve Step program my way.

I was on my fourth sponsor. I met with him and committed to making daily phone calls, attending a minimum of five meetings per week, doing daily SA readings, praying throughout the day, and writing my First Step. I made a list of boundaries I needed to maintain and reported each day to my sponsor and to the meeting how I was doing with my boundaries. I avoided people, places, and things that could lead to acting out and "stuck with the winners."

I am happy to report that through the grace of God and the fellowship of SA, I have been continuously sober since 1993. It has not been easy, but it is certainly worth it! The program works, even for one like me with years of chronic slipping! I'm in awe at the change in my life today. Now when I get tempted, instead of resorting to the old "stinking thinking," I am able to look beyond to the despair, remorse, and consequences that always result. Instead of seeing recovery as a matter of not being able to have sex, I see my recovery as freedom from the imprisonment of lust. My whole life and thinking are continuously being changed day by day.

This program has given me more than I ever dreamed. Besides sobriety today, I have friends in the program who know me for who I really am and support me. At my job, I have earned promotions and leadership roles. I have hobbies and other interests. In the past, all my time was spent acting out, I had no other interests. I can look myself in the mirror today and be proud of who I see.

Today, I want to live.

One of the most treasured gifts I have received from this program besides sobriety is my girlfriend of over five years. Before, I never had a relationship for more than six months; we are planning for marriage. After about two years of dating, seeing that we were becoming committed to each other, I took the risk and told her I was a sexaholic. I wanted to be loved for who I am, not for who I pretended to be. I knew I might lose her if I were honest, yet I was willing to risk it. She was accepting and now attends Twelve Step meetings for herself. We attend couples meetings together, and have a relationship based upon honesty and open communication—for the first time in my life.

SA has saved my life. Better yet, SA has given me a new life. For all of this and for all the people who have made this possible, I am truly grateful. Thank you, SA, for showing me that recovery is possible for me too! I now believe that whether young or old, single or married, sex is indeed optional! As long as I follow the Steps each day to the best of my ability, I know there is nothing to fear. I can finally see that it does get better; we do recover.

26. The Only Way I Knew

When I was a little girl, about five years old, I remember sitting on my grandfather's lap and combing his hair. It gave me such happy, good feelings. My grandfather died when I was seven. From that time on, I had trouble in school. I couldn't concentrate, I would daydream, and I had headaches. I was a lonely child after I lost that special relationship. I didn't know how to get love like that from anyone else, so I comforted myself in my fantasies where I was a fairy princess. My Prince Charming would come and carry me off. We would live in the land of happiness forever doing wonderful deeds and sharing our love.

I was a middle child. My older sister did well in school and was very dependable. My younger sister was very pretty and precocious, so people always gave her a lot of attention. I set out to be all those things my sisters were. I worried about how I looked, and I tried to make lots of friends. I never fit in with the really popular people, but I found I could always have a group of friends by going with the less popular ones. I became very social. When I reached my teens, I found that if I flirted, I could also have lots of boyfriends. The feelings I found from having all this attention were like the feelings I remembered from the days I spent with my grandfather.

Flirting was the only way I knew to communicate with the males in my world. I felt guilty and ashamed for flirting the way I did, but I didn't think I was smart enough to talk about anything that might interest them. I was torn between wanting the attention and feeling guilty about the way I was getting it. I had a secret place between the church and my house where the clover was high. I would sit there and cry for hours. I felt so inadequate and lonely. The more inadequate and lonely I felt, the more my need for attention. The high I got from flirting kept growing. I found that flirting led to petting. Even though I felt high from the sexual feelings and the attention, I would feel even more guilt from my behavior. I would go to my spot and cry from loneliness and guilt.

120

Looking back, I see that I was becoming trapped in a painful downward spiral

When I was seventeen, I met a guy who drank. I had never been out with a guy who drank in front of me. He got drunk on our second date, and I decided then and there that he needed a nice girl like me to help him not to drink so much. He was the first man I had sex with, and I got pregnant. We got married in a big church wedding. He came late and was drunk. I swore I would get a divorce after the baby came, but I didn't.

He was always gone with his drinking buddies. I felt angry and lonely much of the time. I tried to search for the God of my childhood to comfort me, but I didn't know how to find Him. I started flirting again and found I felt better. Flirting became my drug whenever I felt bad.

As the flirting progressed, I started thinking again that there was a Prince Charming out there who would make me feel whole. I progressed from flirting to having affairs. Every time I had an affair, I would fall madly in love. The excitement of the chase was followed by the heartbreak of being used and by obsessing about a person I couldn't have. Guilt, shame, and remorse were feelings I had to cope with every day. I would promise myself I would stop what I was doing, but I couldn't. I was searching constantly for the love I needed, and hating myself for the men, the sex, and not being able to stop. I would pray, and then I would curse God because I couldn't stop; I thought God wasn't listening to me. I felt so hopeless I wanted to die.

I tried taking tranquilizers to stop the pain I was in, but it didn't help. I quit drugs and went to a psychiatrist, who helped me look at my behavior objectively. Many people were doing what I was doing. If so many people were having affairs, it must be normal. I took permission from this rationalization to start searching again for my Prince. Just before coming into recovery, I became obsessed with one man.

I hated being so obsessed and constantly fought for control. This man and I were in a constant battle for supremacy. I could not get enough of him. Lust was so strong it was destroying me. I hated him. I loved him. I needed to please him, but it was never enough. I felt like a junkie ready to come out of my skin when I didn't get a call from him. I hated the way I was living, but I could not stop. I felt so inadequate and alone. I thought I knew what hell would be like. Finally God answered my prayers by showing me a solution. I knew when I first heard about Al-Anon that it held an answer for me. My family situation had become really crazy. I had a daughter who was a drug addict, and my husband was an alcoholic. We went for help, and all of us wound up in different treatment centers. The counselors told me I was going to treatment because I was codependent, but I knew my problem was men and sex. I had tried to stop my sexual behavior most of my life, but I couldn't control it. My problem controlled me.

I worked the Al-Anon program one day at a time in an attempt to control my lust. I continued to flirt with other men. I thought flirting was alright, and my life did seem to be getting better. I didn't have the highs anymore, but I also didn't have the lows. However, I was still having some problems with my feelings.

Then I heard about Sexaholics Anonymous. Right away I knew that I needed this program, but I was afraid of what I would have to surrender. I was on an emotional roller coaster the week before the meeting. At my first Sexaholics Anonymous meeting, I found that my flirting was a high. I would need to stop it if I was to be sexually sober. I learned that flirting and masturbation, followed by guilt, had kept me emotionally stirred up and had prevented me from knowing true recovery. When I became willing to let go, God did his part by relieving me of the obsession. He has given me relief from obsession and spiritual growth since my first day of sobriety in 1983.

God has worked miracles in my life through the Twelve Step programs of recovery. My husband and I are still married. We understand the balance between taking care of ourselves for our marriage and giving of ourselves to the marriage. We have a relationship with God first because that relationship fills the emptiness that we were so frightened of and searching to fill. With the freedom we've found comes the ability to love each other in a new and exciting way. My relationships with my husband, son, and daughter are warm and different and growing all the time.

My husband and I went into business to help recovering people. We put everything we had into that venture, both financially and physically. We trusted God to replenish our resources. We both believed in the recovery process offered by Twelve Step programs. We were dedicated to helping others find their way to these programs. Our daughter was also in recovery and involved in our business. We were able to help others for many years.

We have three wonderful grandchildren whom we see often. I continue to operate my hair dressing business, perhaps in honor of my grandfather. Our only son used to hate me for what I had done. Today he calls me and tells me his problems. I can say that the Promises have come true for me. My family has grown and developed. Fear of economic insecurity has left me. We have grown spiritually. What used to be a life of mistrust has fallen away. I have no regrets and look forward to what each day brings. God has removed much of my selfishness and has given me peace in my belief that I will be taken care of and be given exactly what I need for my spiritual growth. My prayers have been answered because I am taking the steps that allow God to work in my life. I feel that my hopes for finding love and doing good things for others are being fulfilled—one day at a time.

27. The Sweetest Words

"Hi, my name is ----, and I'm a sexaholic."

Those are the sweetest words in the world to me. I've been a sexaholic for over fifty years, but it has only been in the last 15 years that I have been free to talk about it or do something about it. To start at the beginning, I need to say that my parents did the very best they could with the parenting skills handed down to them. I was frail as a child and had all the childhood illnesses twice. I felt I was to blame for the high medical bills. I contracted rheumatic fever and missed half of third grade, all of fifth grade, and part of seventh grade. My bed was moved to the dining room each of those times. I was the freak in everybody's hair. Not even being allowed to walk to the bathroom meant no real privacy for anything.

I was home alone all day, every day, for an entire school year. About this time an older man, a neighbor, started paying a lot of attention to me. Eventually he molested me. It was wonderful to have someone who wanted me. The physical feelings introduced me to a whole new world of excitement. The secrecy of these meetings added to the mystery and intrigue. I now had something new to add to my fantasy world. I was already escaping into the world created by the radio and Saturday matinee. Cowboys, Indians, Royal Canadian Mounted Police, and Tarzan, mixed with comics, made fertile ground for my escape.

Other events added to my acquaintance with sex. My older brother sodomized me. It was a frightening experience, but there was excitement too. About the same time, my father caught a number of us neighborhood boys when we were supposed to be camping outside. We were playing doctor. He sent all the boys home and told me to go to my room. Nothing was ever mentioned about the incident again, so I learned that some things were not to be talked about. Later, when I tried to tell my mother about the molestation that had happened to me, all she heard was something about masturbation and said that everybody does it sometimes and not to worry. Some things were not to be mentioned, ever.

I started hanging around the local park restrooms, went searching for a youth leader I had heard about. When I had my driver's license, I returned to my abuser. My father died when I was in high school, and I became the object of emotional incest by my mother. Masturbation became a regular occurrence: at home, school, church, camp—even driving. Anytime that I was alone became an opportunity to do it, and the riskier, the better. Instead of dating, I wife-shopped and married, but nothing was as good as my fantasies and masturbation. I even told myself that I was not being unfaithful to her because I had never been with another woman since we married. All my extramarital sex was with men.

The guilt of having a secret life was overwhelming. Even with these feelings, I could not stop any of it. God knows I tried. I continued to cross boundaries. Going places and doing things I said I would never do. Buying things I would then throw away, only to dig in the garbage to retrieve. Going to strangers' houses in the middle of the night for anonymous sex. Everything I encountered became fodder for my addiction. Everything had a sexual connotation. Nothing was beyond my perverted activities. Not animal, mineral, or vegetable. My mind was consumed with sex. What I would do, when and where I would do it, with whom or what—all of this was constantly on my mind. And when I was not thinking sex, I was into resentment about the idiots I worked with, the stupid administration, my ungrateful family, or incompetent sales people.

I had three children and two foster children and was not emotionally available for any of them. My marriage ended in divorce. Doctoral studies ended abruptly. I quit my job rather than be fired; I was too hard to get along with, and I was causing problems with the staff. A thousand miles from my children, living alone in unhealthy surroundings, indulging my fantasies—my life was a wreck.

Ten years later I had a job, belonged to a church, was buying a home, and had money in the bank. But I was still miserable, doing the same things and not having fun doing them. Suicide was on my mind much of the time. If only I could figure out a way to do it and still be around to see how sorry they would be when I was gone! I made an appointment with a counselor. At the first session I told things that I had never told anyone, things that had been secrets for more than forty years, everything. I really dumped.

With his help I found a Friday night open meeting of Sexaholics Anonymous. I had to act out before I went to the meeting. The next meeting was Saturday morning, 115 miles away, but I went—and sober. I did not act out on the highway or stop at a rest area. I did not act out getting ready to leave for the meeting. I was sober. The next meeting was on Tuesday, and I was still sober. That was a miracle because Monday night I had to stay in a motel. I did not do any of those crazy things that I always did in motels. One day at a time I was staying sober.

That was in 1990. This program had put me in touch with a Power greater than myself. I had tried to do this on my own, and it had never worked. Through faith in this fellowship and my Higher Power, I was able to accept my first-year medallion. I had a sponsor, worked Steps One through Three, and was working on Four. I attended at least four meetings a week, made coffee when possible, chaired meetings, attended an international convention and two regional retreats, and fellowshipped a lot after meetings. My first-year medallion took 30,000 miles of driving to and from meetings and $180 in turnpike tolls, but it was worth it. I wasn't in pain, wasn't doing things that I didn't want to do. I had made the real connection. I was home.

Where am I now?

> I am not controlled by lust. A thought can come in my mind, and I do not have to do anything about it except to send it away. I have freedom from the obsession, the compulsion.

> I am not proud of my past, but I don't have to hide from it. I can acknowledge it, knowing that it is in the past. In sobriety, I can share that past with other

sexaholics along with the joy of the present time. Nothing I have said in a meeting or with a newcomer has ever come back to bite me.

I can see how sharing my experience with others helps them as well as me. When I share with my sponsees and they with me, there is a hedge around me, protecting my sobriety. Sometimes a sponsee calls me just when I'm thinking I need to make a phone call.

One way I handle problems is to call my sponsor. He often comes up with something I would not have thought of in a hundred years. As a sponsor, I sometimes am amazed at things that I suggest to sponsees. It has to be my Higher Power talking to them and me.

When I first came into the program, I thought that life was boring sometimes. I now understand this to be serenity. I don't have those wild mood swings, those deep depressions, or those adrenaline highs. Life has excitement and variety, but now it is more subtle.

I can now be alone in my house without any TV, radio, or CD playing, alone with God and at peace.

Before, I could only think about me. Now I am remembering birthdays and anniversaries and sending thank-you cards. I have good relations with my children. My grandchildren have only seen me in sobriety.

In recovery, I started a new business. I used up all my savings, and things were tight for a couple of years. To be able to trust my Higher Power to provide took something I learned within these walls. I have been able to pay back some of my savings. I am comfortable giving time and money for worthy causes. I do not expect rewards or a return dollar for dollar.

I let my Higher Power direct what I was trying to direct. It works out so much better this way. In my disease I would sometimes say, "Hey God, we've got three choices, and I really want the first one." He would say, "Are you sure?" "Yes, I am sure." When He would give me that choice, it would usually turn out badly. When I came into SA I learned that I could say, "Hey God, just for today, I will let You make the choices." And God would respond, "I'm so glad you finally let me choose. You know that time that you gave me three choices? I had 672 other choices for you. You only saw three of them, and they were the bottom three on the list."

Over the period of my recovery, I have had to look at every single thing in my life and ask, "Is this true, is this appropriate, is it relevant for my life today?" I am amazed at the trash that has been weeded out of my life and the flowers that have bloomed.

Yes, God is doing great things for me—when I let him. I am able to travel the world, see strange and wondrous things, and meet some very special people. I am doing things that I never dreamed of doing. I don't have to do things on my own anymore.

28. I Am Insane, Not Evil

I am a grateful recovering sexaholic and an orthodox Jew. I have been obsessed with sex and lust almost as long as I can remember. I recall, at age twelve, sitting in the bathroom in Israel, playing with myself. By age thirteen I was masturbating compulsively.

My father died when I was eight. As a result, my mother felt she had to be the father in our home. She was strict and held extremely high expectations for me both morally and academically. For example, she taught me that I was a bad person if I slept more than five or six hours a night, so I rarely enjoyed adequate rest. The atmosphere in my boyhood home was one of extremely rigorous religious observance. I believed that I was committing an enormous sin by acting out. After each bout I felt very guilty and promised myself I would stop, but soon I would act out again, always again. I figured I was sinning anyway, so I could sin a little more.

At age twelve I was pushed two years ahead of my classmates into high school, a private yeshiva ruled by an iron-fisted uncle. Since my high school was a boarding school I slept in a dorm. One Friday night during the first semester a much older boy raped me. He did it again the following week. Later, the rapist took me aside and tried to talk to me about what he had done to me. I denied that anything had happened. Over my denial, he told me that if I ever told anyone, two things would happen: first, we would be blacklisted, blocking me from attending any good school in the future; second, he would kill himself, and his blood would be on my hands.

My schoolwork, which had always been excellent, began sinking. By the second semester my grades began to decline and I was skipping classes. I coped with my scholastic failure and my family's shame by retreating even further into lust and fantasy.

At fourteen, having emigrated to the United States, I began cruising the city streets looking at women, riding the subways for hours at night, sidling up to female strangers. I was skipping school to be out on the streets. Even when I was in class, my mind was elsewhere. I spent hours at the windows of the school looking across campus at women in their homes. Only my mother's frantic string-pulling kept me from being expelled any number of times for not doing the work.

My strict religious upbringing taught me that my acting out was a grievous sin and that G-d would punish me severely. My intense guilt did not stop me. It pushed me further into fantasy and lust, into myself. I was convinced G-d hated me. In my self-hate I acted out in nonsexual ways, like stealing money and merchandise. I lost interest in my religious training and became disconnected from G-d as I had once understood Him.

At age sixteen I confided this secret world of mine—with all its shame and remorse—to some of my religious leaders. The rabbis told me that my acting out was very wrong and that G-d would punish me severely. They sternly warned me to amend my evil ways. When I heard their words, I hated myself even more vehemently than before and lost all hope of ever attaining self-esteem.

One of the rabbis gave me his telephone number to call when I wanted to act out. I called him a few times, but I did not reach out to him consistently when I was tempted. He asked me why. I was too ashamed to admit that hearing him tell me how evil my acts were only drove me deeper into lusting, sexing, and stealing.

Before long, I pursued my lust across the gender line. The idea of sex with a man repelled me, but I did it anyway. I had sex every week or so with a college schoolmate—swearing off it after each episode and avoiding him until the next time we acted out. I hated same-sex acting out worse than any of my other lust acts, but my hatred couldn't bring me to stop. My college sex partner told a rabbi about us. I was referred to a rabbi-counselor who told me marriage would channel my urges in healthier, saner directions. So at age nineteen I married the second girl I ever dated. It was a marriage arranged according to our traditions. She was my first female sex partner, and she saved me . . . for about three weeks. We were well matched, and we enjoyed building a home together, but she wasn't enough. I had to have more. Sex with my wife had opened the door to my next step down—prostitutes. I acted out with every kind of prostitute, from high-class call girls to skinny, strung-out streetwalkers. I loved the danger.

When I was married I planned to finish my rabbinical studies in four to five years, but my absenteeism got me kicked out of a succession of schools. I bought a car to have easier and faster access to prostitutes. I would disappear from the house for hours, telling my wife later that the car had broken down or making up some other excuse. I was back to cruising city streets and frequenting X-rated movies and peep shows. I visited the bath houses. One night, while I was cruising in the middle of winter, someone stole my shoes and I had to make my way home in my stocking feet.

During the High Holy Days I left my in-laws' house supposedly to visit a rabbi. That day as I was soliciting prostitutes, a pimp threw me out of my car and stole it. The police recovered the car and notified me. When my father-in-law and I went to the station to reclaim it, the sergeant told us the driver was claiming it as payment for sex.

I started making religious promises to myself like, "If I masturbate, I will fast for the rest of the day." I slept on my bedroom floor to atone for acting out. In a year's time all that my attempts at atonement accomplished was to annoy and upset my wife.

My only thought was gratification, never consequences—until afterward. After every encounter, I promised myself I would stop. I hoped a psychotherapist would help me find my ideal sexual outlet. I was still convinced that I would be satisfied once I found the perfect match.

And my insanity continued. Somehow I always had a story for my wife. I had been held up in traffic, had forgotten my license and been stopped by the police—whatever I could think of to cover the truth. My sudden disappearances terrified my wife, yet I yelled at her for rounding up the family to look for me. "Don't you know your own husband already?" I demanded angrily. "I was just taking a walk!"

By my mid-twenties my acting out was so draining that I could not show up for work reliably and soon could not hold a steady job. So I decided to go into business for myself. But here too I flagged. I missed appointments. I did not put in the hours the business required. I was too busy acting out. The only career I pursued with real energy was scheming new ways to escape into sex. My career was lust. I began using household money to act out. I borrowed against my credit cards and spent the money on prostitutes. My credit was ruined.

One night, on a trip to another city with my family to obtain medical testing for my son, I left my family in a motel and went cruising. Here was a new city! I had to sample the prostitutes. I was arrested by an undercover policeman and spent half the night in a holding cell with three dozen drunks and vagrants who urinated on the floor. After a few hours I was moved to a small two-man cell. Sitting there, going back over my life, I felt more sober than I had in years. I swore off my sex addiction for good—again. After my release and another story for my wife, I slept through my son's hospital visiting hours and scored a call girl.

Soon lust made me so reckless that I started cruising my own suburban area. People from my congregation saw me with the girls, and my rabbi gave me a lecture. Business associates saw me haggling with prostitutes and word got around. I knew I was ruining my reputation as a businessman and a good Jew, but danger was part of my high.

My son was born with severe cerebral palsy. He is a cripple for life. He was born the day after one of my all-night sex binges following a month in Israel during which I spent ten thousand dollars on prostitutes. I believed my son's illness was G-d's punishment for my acting out. For a time I stayed home and I was abstinent. But soon I was back out there.

By age thirty I was using alcohol and cocaine to intensify my lust binges with prostitutes; at thirty-three I was a full-blown crack addict, stealing from my wife's purse, from my twelve-year-old daughter, and from my business associates to pay for my prostitutes and drugs. I swore on the Torah in synagogue that I would stop drugging and sexing. It never even slowed me down. My business was failing; fellow businessmen knew what I was and would not deal with me.

I was spending thousands of dollars a month. I passed bad checks throughout my Jewish community, turning friends of many years against me. I became too ashamed to show my face in synagogue. I skipped daily prayers. I stopped answering the phone.

In 1991 I took my wife and my son to another town for three days while he underwent surgery. I took no money, hoping that would keep me from prostitutes. Within hours after arriving I had my book-keeper wire me $500, and when that ran out I cashed another $125 in bad checks with a rabbi. I spent scant minutes in the hospital with my son. I had lost all semblance of self-respect. I was out of control, and I did not know how to stop. I found Alcoholics Anonymous through a counselor, but still could not stop drinking, drugging, and lusting.

One night, desperate after a binge of alcohol and lust, I called an AA member. I told him everything. I told him about my inability to achieve at school, my overeating, my compulsive masturbation, and the progression that had brought me to despair. I believed not only that I was a failure at life, but also that I was evil.

He responded by saying something that has stayed with me. You are not evil, he said, but sick—insane, in fact. The solution was nei-ther to punish myself nor to resign myself to my active addiction as G-d's punishment. But G-d could help me. Something clicked. I am insane, not evil. Since that night I have been sober from alcohol and drugs.

But I was still insane with lust. Celebrating my first AA anniver-sary, I went to my old cruising haunts. I was terrified. This was the way back to crack and booze in a hurry. When I got up the nerve to tell my AA sponsor about it, he told me to satiate my lust with mas-turbation and pornography but to stay away from prostitutes.

I continued to masturbate and stay sober from alcohol. But my lust did not sit still. With thirteen months of AA sobriety, I found myself cruising to pick up a prostitute again. I knew that acting out with a prostitute would lead me back to alcohol and drugs, and I knew that if I picked up alcohol and drugs again, I would die. Somehow I got home without acting out. It was clear to me then that lust was my drug and that I had to find a support group for my lust or I would die. I remember the day in 1992 when I contacted SA. It is still my sexual sobriety date. I surrendered completely to G-d and the SA program. I followed directions from my sponsor a day at a time. I knew that I must never forget that I am insane.

I began to comprehend the depths of my insanity when I started working the Fourth through Ninth Steps. The Ninth Step was very painful for me because it reminded me of all the people I have hurt. It also meant a prison sentence for grand larceny because of one of my fund-raising schemes for prostitutes and drugs.

I am not able to make direct amends to most of the people I used and hurt through lust, yet I hold myself ready to do so. In G-d's time I will be given the opportunity to make amends to those people. The Tenth Step reminds me that I am insane, especially when I trip over my chief character defects: anger, resentment, fear, and self-pity. Today G-d makes it possible to find a different, better, and happier way of life.

I have worked the Eleventh Step—prayer and meditation—since the day I got sexually sober. The Twelfth Step—working with others—is the strongest medicine of all, especially when I am caught up in self-pity. The days of miracles are still with us. There is a Power outside myself, greater than myself, which is ready, willing, and able to give me hourly and daily reprieves from my addictions. That One is G-d. I am a short-tempered, resentful, jealous, lazy person, and in all these ways my life is unmanageable. But if I surrender to Him, He has proven to me He will stretch out His arms to me every minute, every hour. Sometimes I still struggle against the old feeling that I am not a good Jew. But G-d shows me that I am a good and caring person. I am grateful to be a sober member of SA, knowing that I am only insane, not evil, and that G-d will take care of me.

29. Accepting Imperfection

I had always felt less than others, like I had no right to be forgiven when I made mistakes, like I did not deserve anything good to happen to me. I grew up in a family where sex was a forbidden topic and where I was chastised for expressing anything not acceptable to my parents. I discovered masturbation at an early age. Between the ages of twelve and fourteen, my older brother used me as a sexual outlet. I so wanted his affection and approval that I didn't realize that I was being abused. Only after I came into SA and heard other women's stories did I realize that the situation was inappropriate.

In my teen years, romantic fantasy was my obsession. Though it's normal for adolescent girls to have crushes on movie stars, professional athletes, or musicians, what started out as a fascination with teen magazines turned into an elaborate fantasy life, with film stars and athletes filling my thoughts, asleep and awake. I loved to read from an early age, and I was especially drawn to stories with romantic themes. Later I hunted down and found books with erotic scenes. I thought I wouldn't need any of this anymore when I got a real live boyfriend.

In my junior high years I was not one of the cute, attractive, popular girls. It was painful to be on the outside of what appeared to be the important crowd (I remember thinking that it was no wonder I wasn't wanted, I was too ugly). I longed for attention from boys. Again, I went beyond the normal crushes on boys that teen girls experience. At thirteen, I pursued the object of my fantasy; I started following a boy home from school and calling his house until his mother told me to leave him alone. I just went on to being obsessed with someone else.

At this point the yearning was not so much sexual as emotional/romantic, a need for approval, a desire to be wanted. At sixteen, I lost weight and grew my hair; I felt more self-confident, more like I fit in. I hit the jackpot with my first boyfriend—at least that is how it felt. It was my first experience of the Big Fix. It was a high like I had never felt before. I had my first sexual experiences with him, and it was then I started to see my sexuality as my power. If I could look good and make a guy interested in me, I thought, I could keep him by satisfying his sexual needs. I did not realize that what I needed was a spiritual connection; after fast starts, these "relationships" failed again and again. What I needed was connection, and my emptiness and hollowness usually became apparent to the boy a few weeks after we started to date. For years, I followed this pattern over and over with the same results. The relationship would start with a high and end with the boy sick of me—and me feeling crushed and abandoned. I never learned from these situations, although I tried to. In college, I started what I now know was stalking—following men on the campus, sending them love letters and gifts, and finding out things about their personal lives. I acted out with almost anyone who was interested. Later in my twenties, I started to date more than one man at a time in case any of them "fell through"—so I would always have someone. And the more this happened, the more urgent my yearning for connection became.

This is when my addiction really took off. I started answering and putting personal ads into a local alternative newspaper and met a number of men that way. I invited these men into my home, met them at their homes, acted out with them. I had no concern for my physical health or safety. I met one man on the bus and another in a laundromat and, again, went out with them and acted out with them without a second thought. I thought masturbation was not a problem, was not out of control; but I never went more than a few days without it, and I used it in inappropriate places like public rest room stalls and my car. I fed my lust with erotic novels and movies.

But the most intense part of my addiction was the romantic part; sex was a way to draw someone in and possibly fill my emotional needs. Getting into a relationship was what gave me a wonderful feeling of power, but in fact I was not in control and I wasn't powerful. I had given the power to all those men I acted out with.

I did not know what real intimacy meant. When I met my husband I had just broken off with yet another failed relationship. My husband was a good man, who treated me well and loved me for my sense of humor, kindness, intelligence—not because I could do something for him sexually. I almost let him go out of my life because I thought that he couldn't possibly be what I was looking for—there was no "chemistry," no magic connection. I didn't know how to be in a give-and-take relationship based on real life. With my husband's help, and the grace of my Higher Power, I stayed with him and married him. One of the thoughts I had frequently during our engagement was that I would never be able to go out with anyone else again—which felt scary.

After marriage, I couldn't admit to myself that it wasn't normal that I developed crushes on some of my husband's friends and continued masturbating and fantasizing about movie stars or other public figures. Our sexual relationship floundered—I was put off by his interest in me. A few years went by, and I had my first child. I took a leave from my job and then went back a year or so later.

This was the turning point in my addiction. My lust and romantic longing erupted. Within a month I was stalking a man at work and putting my job at risk by my lack of attention to it and by my not-very-well-hidden behavior. These were boundaries that I had never broken before. My obsession with this man was overpowering, and although I tried to intrigue with him, he was married and was not a sexaholic. I put tremendous emotional energy and time into trying to seduce him. When this did not work, I found another man in my office who was more than willing to intrigue with me, including some physical activity in his office during the working day. I did not even like this second man, but I was driven to act out with him. The emptiness in me was a chasm. Each time, acting out made me want more, and do more dangerous things. Later, my first sponsor in SA told me that as long as I continued acting out, there would always have to be a next "hit," that I would never be satisfied, that in fact all of these men were interchangeable. My flings were not about intimacy or true union but a manifestation of a need that would never be filled with acting out.

My worst episode, my bottom, came when my husband left on a business trip. I had sex in our home with my husband's friend, with our three-year-old sleeping upstairs. I was convinced that my husband and I just weren't compatible, and I had to be "free" to pursue my needs. I was on the verge of separating from him and giving up being with my son full-time. I should say again that my husband was a faithful, kind, and loving man, and a good father. I was blinded by the wave of addiction that had come over me and the belief that intimacy meant constant romantic and sexual excitement. My spirit was corrupted—I could not have a relationship with myself, as I could never be at peace.

I came to SA out of desperation. After that last episode, I had an emotional breakdown—unable to eat, sleep, or function. I couldn't bear the fact that this lust partner and I were not going to be able to pursue a relationship, and my husband had found out that there was some intrigue between us (although he didn't know the full story). I wasn't upset about hurting my husband; rather, I was devastated that my "chemistry" with this man had been frustrated and that I would never get to act out with him again. Talk about the unreal! It was a time in my life when I don't know how I got from day to day. But that was what brought me to my first SA meeting.

I had to admit and accept, at least for twenty-four hours, that my habit had conquered me. Withdrawing from the habit was possible only by coming to meetings and staying in constant contact with a sponsor and other sober women in SA. It took me another year to really get the program because I thought I could do half measures—still flirt, still dress to be noticed, still pursue old relationships—and still be alright. That did not work. Finally, one day in 1993, I had to stop cold. No sex with myself or others—and no sex with my husband for a time. My Higher Power blessed me with a job opportunity that took me away from the poisoned environment I had created with my acting out. It was all frightening. Without the "freedom" of acting out, I felt as though my life was over. I remember feeling like I was jumping off a cliff, but I knew that the pain of continuing down the path I had been traveling would be worse than the pain of quitting. Instead, my life eventually moved away from fantasy and toward reality. I was freed from obsession.

Without SA meetings and the support of sober members, both men and women, I would never have been able to stop and stay stopped. Just the stopping part took a lot of working the program and constantly reaching out for help. It was a tough withdrawal—which I later realized was a clear sign of the extent of my addiction. My First Step, read to my sponsor, was filled with painful details about the many situations I had gotten myself into. Telling all of this to her brought freedom. It brought acceptance and a hand to guide me toward an understanding of my past. I finally started recognizing the damage that acting out had done to me and to others. My husband was not to blame for my problems—in fact, he had been willing to do anything in his power to keep us together. Even when he found out about me and his friend, once I was in SA and he saw that I was trying hard to turn my life around, he was willing to stay with me. Since then, I have been in the process of trying to right my wrongs. Paying attention to others, and allowing for their imperfections, has probably been one of the hardest things to learn in sobriety. Real intimacy and true union are not constantly exciting. Love and intimacy come from taking the actions of love, which means acting in a loving way even though I don't feel like it. This kind of true union gives me the real connection and makes me feel that I am home with myself. I do feel today that I am in my spiritual home. After thirteen years of sexual sobriety, twenty years of marriage, and two beautiful children (my second child, a daughter, was conceived and born in sobriety), I am grateful and often in a state of wonder at the satisfaction that this sober life gives me.

I stay sexually sober today by staying close to the program. In the second year of my sobriety, this addiction reared its ugly head again and I was close to leaving the program, thinking that I could handle things on my own. It's incredible to think I could forget all that I had been through, but I know that is the nature of addiction. A woman who does not have this addiction can have an innocuous admiration for a man; for me it can turn into a lust obsession, with space taken up in my mind with images of him and mental voyeurism about his sexual life. I don't get into conversations with other women when they are talking about attractive men. I don't have "men friends." My husband is my friend, and I have a wealth of friends who are women.

Thank God for my sponsor who sets me straight. I work the Steps in my life every day. My daily First Step is admitting my powerlessness, including turning over lustful thoughts or incidents to my sponsor. Working the Steps helps me make fewer mistakes that I have to make amends for. When I make mistakes, I can make the amends because I know that I'm human and that I will be imperfect. This makes it easier for me to accept my husband and other members of my family and their imperfections. I can feel some peace of mind, and I am in touch with myself and my spirit. Each day I maintain the connection between my Higher Power and myself through prayer and meditation. I attend meetings as often as I am able to, and I tell my story whenever I can. I reach out to newcomer women especially, because I do not forget how bewildered and scared I felt at my first meetings, which were almost all men. I am a sponsor and I am sponsored. I am obligated—and I take the obligation willingly—to help others find sobriety; the best defense I have against acting out is to work with another sexaholic.

30. Getting "Me" out of the Way

I had little or no interest in sex until about age twelve, when I began to experiment sexually along with other boys, looking at pornography and masturbating. In high school I began being sexual with my first steady girlfriend, who stopped me from "going all the way." When I was in eleventh grade and going steady with the girl I planned to marry upon graduation, we went all the way and lust began to work overtime in my life.

As it turned out, we didn't marry. I joined the Air Force and married a different hometown girl who took the time to write to me while I was alone and away from home. It was a long-distance love affair that grew more out of my loneliness and romantic fantasies than from an actual relationship. We had sex when I went home on leave. That sealed my fate. I asked her to marry me, and she said yes. I wanted sex, and she wanted to get away from home. That was not a good foundation for marriage. I didn't know that I was a sexaholic and that I had many years of insanity yet before me.

We were hardly married when I was sent on a cross-county flight to a border town. I went across the border to get a prostitute, the first of many. Soon I was going to prostitutes on the streets of the city where we lived. Our marriage began to flounder.

At the time, I thought I was being cool and sophisticated. My drinking became chronic. I started taking prescription drugs to cope with long working schedules, my hatred of the military, and my guilt from acting out with prostitutes and to numb my feelings over my extramarital affairs. Once out of the military, I began doing things that were illegal. I no longer felt cool and sophisticated, but perverted and sick. My problems became more than my wife could tolerate. She took our two sons and daughter and divorced me.

After my failure at marriage, I got drunk and tried to commit suicide. When I failed, I tried to find solace in God and my church; but it appeared to me that by my church's laws I would have to spend the rest of my life single and celibate. So I left God, my church, and the state where I lived for another state. I buried myself in work and celebrated my new freedom with booze and prostitutes. I was free, free from the laws of God, religion, and marriage. I called myself an atheist and vowed that no one would ever hurt me again. I joined the swinging singles until I met and married my second wife. She already had two children by a previous marriage. I was not committed to that marriage, either.

My sexaholism, alcoholism, and drug addiction took a drastic turn for the worse about a year into that marriage. I decided to quit my job, sell our house, and take my new family to a tropical island to find my true calling as an artist. We returned after a few months with one painting I had done, but I could say that I had lived like Gauguin. I had also acquired a taste for rum and marijuana. Because of my degenerating state of mind and irresponsible behavior, we lost all our savings. We lived on welfare while I painted, drank, got stoned, and lusted after my five-year-old stepdaughter.

I got involved in the illegal drug trade to support my drug addiction. I was hunted by law enforcement agencies in two countries. I barely escaped prosecution. My lifestyle continued to deteriorate, and I tried to commit suicide a second time. My wife rushed me to the hospital. The doctor only looked at me in disgust and told my wife I wasn't going to die.

During this time I was bringing up my children and stepchildren in a rustic cabin without utilities of any kind, using rainwater for washing. I was modeling the criminal lifestyle for them, growing marijuana to sell and dealing cocaine to the other growers. I had my two older children (the oldest boy had escaped into the military) help me grow the pot and the two younger stepchildren sold it at school. Finally, I caught a glimpse of the abyss awaiting me. This was the day I almost shot my son in a violent rage because he dared to defy me. My mind was telling me that I had real power if I could kill my own son, but I heard a faint voice telling me not to.

I will eternally bless that voice and that day because that was the stopping-point for me—I had finally hit my bottom. I left the cabin and went out into the forest to get away for a time to think. In my utter despair I turned back to the God I had abandoned years before and asked for help. There weren't any flashes of light or a voice thundering down from the heavens, but I felt a peace and I knew somehow that my life would get better.

I tried to return to legitimate employment, but I was unable to hold a job. I tried church and faith healers, but I didn't get healed. I continued to use alcohol and drugs and to act our sexually. I began reading the Bible, but in my mental state I began to think I was the second coming of Christ; I was even getting a following of drunks and addicts to preach to. I decided to ask God what to do next. I was sure God was going to send me out among the masses (all dressed up in a white outfit). Instead I wound up in the VA drug rehabilitation ward. By the grace of God I have stayed sober from booze and drugs from that day. My battle with lust addiction was not yet over.

I did my Fourth and Fifth Steps with a wonderful God-centered VA analyst over a period of five years, uncovering all my character defects, including my sexual misconduct. He knew nothing about Sexaholics Anonymous—few professionals did at that time. I continued to be plagued by lust. In my early AA sobriety, I granted my second wife the divorce she wanted. I married a younger woman I had met at work who thought I was what she was looking for. I immediately took her hostage for my sex addiction and used her as an object for my lust, although at the time I thought she was my true love and that God had given her to me for being sober in AA. That marriage was doomed. Within a year she left me, and I tried for the third time to commit suicide. I had decided to tell God face to face what I thought of Him and the horrible job He was doing with my life since I'd turned it over to Him.

Once again I wound up in the rehab ward. I was sober in AA, but I still had a long way to go before I would understand what emotional sobriety is. As a result of years of drug abuse, alcoholism, and my suicide attempt, I suffered a cerebral hemorrhage that damaged my brain and put me on permanent Social Security.

During the early years on disability, I remarried my second wife, hoping once again that something or someone would fix me. My lust problem had not gone away, and marriage didn't save me from it. I turned once again to pornography, masturbation, and lusting after other women. I felt the despair of knowing I was hooked and couldn't stop. I knew our marriage would not last this time either. I heard about Sexaholics Anonymous in an AA meeting, so I contacted SA and started going to meetings.

I managed to stay sober for the next three years. As the time of my sobriety began to add up, I began to get self-righteous and intolerant of slippers. I couldn't understand why they couldn't get sober and stay sober like me. At home I wasn't doing any better in my marriage. I was trying to force my wife to confront *her* character defects, but she wasn't having any part of it. I read the SA manual over and over, but I didn't relate to it. My wife got fed up again and suggested she might be happier alone. I felt the same but for a different reason. I had decided that if I were single, I could rise to greater heights of spirituality. Somehow God would ordain me as His Chosen One.

When I perceived what celibacy really meant, I began to blame God again for messing up my life. Why was He punishing me when I was being so good? After all, I reasoned, He created me, so it wasn't my fault. Why should I have to pay for His mistakes? As the resentments continued to build, I avoided meetings because I couldn't stand hearing members with long-term sobriety talk so gleefully about how God was doing for them what they could not do for themselves. I would become very angry at their talk about their gratitude to God for their sobriety because of my resentment against God for not healing me. I am amazed that I stayed sober for as long as I did. I lost my SA sobriety within six months of the time my wife left me. It was all God's fault, so I decided to try staying sober in AA without God.

I moved to get away from my problems. As the saying goes, "Wherever you go, there you are!" I was the problem and nothing changed. I married my fourth wife—my fifth marriage—but my lust addiction soon put an end to that one too. I had only my lust to keep me company.

I started going to other sexual recovery program meetings so that I wouldn't have to swallow my pride and return to SA. My sick reasoning only made me more miserable. Finally, I had to deflate my ego and prepare to slither back into SA and face the humiliation I was sure would come. Instead I was welcomed back as an old friend who had just returned from a long trip.

This time I had no illusions about what I needed to do: surrender my life to God or die. I knew that I had to work Step Three without reservations of any kind. I had to turn my will and my life over to the care of God. I had to turn over my sex life, my disability income, my plans for what I thought my future should be, my children's lives, everything. After trying my best to control and enjoy lust, I finally became willing to give it all to God. That was in the year 1993. As I grew in genuine SA sobriety, I began to understand that I had never been able to see women and girls as people. I always had a hidden agenda for every woman and girl I met.

I had to practice giving over to God every woman I saw and seeing each one as a person separate from gender, as a child of God in need of spiritual love. I began to *really* read and understand what the SA manual and SA members with long-term sobriety had been trying to tell me all along. Now I see that it is not about me, my, and mine. It is about giving of myself to others in spiritual love and service. I work at practicing the St. Francis prayer by becoming a channel of God's love to whomever I meet. I listen with an open mind and heart. I do not have to have an answer. I benefit most when God's love goes through me to the person I am helping. Before, I waited for God to fill me with His love so that I would have some to give away. It doesn't work that way. I have to step out in faith and be of service without the hidden agenda of looking for rewards and acknowledgment. When I do manage to get "me" out of the way, I am blessed ten-fold. I know what is in store for me when I surrender, so I tend to work all the harder to live by spiritual principles rather than my own self-will.

I involve myself in doing SA and AA service work and volunteer work in the community. I am hoping to work someday, to be self-supporting. I had tried to go back to school for retraining several times, but each time I became overwhelmed and dropped out.

I would have had to swallow my pride and apply as a disabled person so that I could get help in completing the courses. Once again I have had to become one of "them" instead of the hip, slick, cool dude who had it all together. (Was I ever?)

When I am willing to let go and let God, He will do for me what I cannot do for myself. I made a mess of everything when I tried to do what I thought God wanted me to do. I was afraid that what God wanted for me would be something I would not want. I am learning what it means to trust that what God wants for me is far better than anything I could ever dream of. I am beginning to understand what the old timers have been telling me about moving from fear-driven sobriety into God-centered sobriety.

Thank You, God, for Sexaholics Anonymous, especially for those sober members who have shown me how to "trudge the road of happy destiny" free from the bondage of lust.

31. No More Excuses

I woke up this morning thanking God. I prayed this simple prayer: "God grant that I may love Thee always and follow Thy will. Do with me according to Thy will." I did my daily readings. This is a day in sobriety. It wasn't always that way. I used to pray, "Oh God, please get me out of this one, and I promise I'll never do it again." Or, "Oh God, if only I had $50,000, I could pay off my debts, make a down payment on a second car for my wife, and buy new clothes for our children. Then everything would be okay." These are called "jail house prayers." I found out about them the hard way.

I was abused as a child. Before my first communion, at age six, my great aunt was sexually abusing me. Even then I knew that no means no, but she ignored my pleas. During the next ten years a minister and youth leader abused me. These experiences became my excuse to act out sexually in a reckless, dangerous, and criminal manner that led to my three-year prison term.

I was fourteen years old when I first abused an eleven-year-old girl. She was my victim: she said no, but I ignored her plea. Between her and the last victim, there were many others. I was fifty-five years old when I engaged in my last sex crime. It was with an eleven-year-old boy. That crime sent me to prison.

After I was arrested, I spent six days in the county lockup. It was Christmas season, and my sisters, who never stopped loving me and stood by me through this whole process, posted $10,000 bail so that I could be with them for the holidays and continue working. I acted out on New Year's Eve.

Gut-wrenching fear and panic set in as I made my first court appearance January 2. It was a cold day outside and inside me. I was scared. I didn't want to go to prison. On my lawyer's advice, I began walking the straight and narrow. "Don't get caught doing anything now," he said. Out of fear, my first period of sexual sobriety began that day.

Because of lengthy delays and legal ploys by my lawyer, I was able to plea bargain with the court system. Exactly ten months after my first court appearance, I was found guilty of sodomy and child abuse and sentenced to one-and-a-half to four years in a maximum security prison. I could have received a sentence of six to eighteen years.

In the crazy three years in prison that followed, much happened to the man who had become a lust-driven predator, who wallowed in self-pity, denial, self-justification, and rationalization, and had plenty of excuses for not getting sexually sober. Sobriety was a familiar word to me when I went to prison because I already had years of AA sobriety. Sexual sobriety was as alien to me as life on Mars. I didn't have a clue. My heart wasn't in it. White knuckling and fear kept me from acting out while I was in prison.

I survived a meaningless prison existence by becoming a law clerk. After I was turned down for parole at my first hearing, I realized that I had to do something to help myself. There were men in prison secretly reading SA material, so I obtained an address from that literature. I wrote and received a free SA manual and brochure from SA Central Office.

Along with this information was a list of people I could write. The member who answered my letter saved me from an unfulfilled life, the mental ward, life in prison, and death. His letter to me was frightfully candid and lacking in fear. In that initial letter, he wrote on company stationery containing not only the company address and phone number, but also his home phone number. He never questioned my behavior, my being in prison, or the circumstances that brought me there. He only talked about himself and this wonderful program called Sexaholics Anonymous. I was intrigued not only about what kind of man this was, but even more about what kind of program this was. "Wow," I said to myself, "where did all this courage come from?"

For the first time in my life, I was willing to listen—the first miracle! I was also willing to follow directions—the second miracle! In the fifteen months that followed, I worked my Twelve Steps for the first time. A loving God was starting to express himself through me. As the axiom goes, "When the student is ready, the teacher will appear!"

During the months of writing from prison, I gained many insights into my affliction. I wanted what I saw in my sponsor, and I was ready to go to any lengths to get it. At first I thought that my years in AA would be a big asset. Wrong! I had to relearn the Steps and make a new application as it specifically addressed my lust addiction. Ten years earlier I had quit—one day at a time—drinking, smoking, overeating, and gambling. They were outside of me. Lust was a part of me. So I tried hard to work a program of sobriety in prison. I tried to look at myself objectively. At my conditional release date, four years to the day after my conviction, I thought I was ready for freedom. I had so much yet to learn.

Church friends arrived at the appointed time to pick me up and give me shelter in their homes. I was fully convinced that Sexaholics Anonymous was the way for me to go—that I needed this fellowship and its sobriety definition. I had a meeting list and phone numbers to call. But the relief of being out of prison—and only those who have been there can understand what that relief is—distracted me. I was in a safe home with some church friends. I didn't have people banging on my cell at three o'clock in the morning saying, "Move so I can see you move," and shining a flashlight in my eyes. I didn't have to go through all the rules and regulations, the formations, and the standing at my gate to be counted. I didn't feel that I needed a meeting or phone calls to SA members.

Ten days after my release, a group of friends invited me to join them on a trip to the mall. I did not know what a grievous mistake that would be. I went gladly. The sights, sounds, and aromas took their toll on me. That night, alone in my room, I acted out. Within seconds I began to weep. I saw with absolute clarity that I could not stay sober alone. I needed the meetings and support of SA.

Five days later I went to my first SA meeting, fully intending to lie about my sobriety date. The first person to give his litany at that Wednesday noon meeting stopped me in my tracks. He admitted to having only three days of sobriety. I found myself admitting to my real sobriety date. The God of my understanding had compelled me to speak the truth. At that meeting I asked an old-timer to be my sponsor and only mildly balked when he asked me to write out the Steps again, even though I had written them in prison.

Since then I have held service positions in local meetings and intergroup. My heart belongs to the service work of the SA Correctional Facilities Committee (SACFC). I've attended meetings in two state prisons and visited inmates in three other prisons in my state. I've attended prison meetings in two other states. Corresponding with over twenty inmates keeps me busy. My involvement with the SACFC has been both fruitful and rewarding. It helps keep me sober. For this I am grateful.

I used to hate the entire church and all its officials and members for the actions of one man. Today, the scared little child who was once abused by a youth leader and a minister has a priest as a sponsor. God has also blessed me with two sponsees, one of whom is in jail on his way to state prison. He was a priest. I have only compassion and love for all my brothers and sisters in SA, regardless of their religious background, color, or other differences. I cannot judge anyone else. I cannot say, "Because he's done this, or she's done that, we have to exclude them from our fellowship."

God's healing and forgiving love is boundless. Thanks to what the God of my understanding has done for me, I am now able to visit my daughter and have lunch with my grandchildren. I abused this daughter when she was twelve, but God has healed our relationship.

When I entered Sexaholics Anonymous in 1996, God did not ask me what my bottom was. God asked me, "Do you want to be sober? Do you want to be restored to sanity? Are you willing to admit that you are powerless over lust and that your life is unmanageable?" I answered yes, and I have been delivered.

God and SA have returned me, a low-bottom pedophile, to sanity, by reinforcing in me that every time I come to a meeting and don't act out, I've done the right thing. God, who allows my presence in SA, is a hope for all who want to stop lusting and become sexually sober, no matter what they have done. In my life, God has given me three essential concepts: wisdom, courage, and serenity. God has given me the wisdom to follow him, the courage to forgive myself and others, and the serenity of living sober in SA.

I borrowed this prayer from a bread wrapper. It is an old prayer, but a good one. I hope God never allows me to forget these words:

> This is the beginning of a new day.
> God has given me this day to use as I will.
> I can waste it, or use it for good.
> What I do today is important because
> I am exchanging a day of my life for it.
> When tomorrow comes,
> this day will be gone forever,
> leaving in its place something
> I have traded it for. I want it to be gain, not loss;
> good, not evil; success, not failure,
> in order that I shall not regret
> the price I paid for it.

32. Lessons Learned

From my earliest recollections at age four, I obsessed over nude women. Any woman I encountered was automatically visualized in the nude. This was true for strangers, relatives, and even the nuns who taught me in elementary school.

At puberty, I discovered masturbation, and my nude visualizations were transformed into sex fantasies. Masturbation and sex fantasy were compulsive from the start, and my two-part illness—obsession and compulsion—was complete.

I continued to masturbate and fantasize throughout my adolescence. At age twenty-one, I got married. With sex built into my life, I thought, I would be cured. Of course, that didn't work.

My obsession and compulsion continued for the fifteen years of that marriage. The marriage ended when I decided that I had the wrong wife. If only I had the right wife, I would be cured. So I left my wife and seven children, got a divorce, and married a second wife, who would fix me. That didn't work.

The problem was me, not my wives, but it would be many more years until I came to that understanding. So, after thirteen years in my second marriage, I decided that I made the same mistake twice. If I really had the right wife, I would be okay. Again, I left my second wife and two more children, got another divorce, and married a third wife.

Not only was I not cured, but I was getting progressively worse. What had been mostly kept secret from my first two wives became more and more apparent. My third wife took me to counselors, therapists, and psychiatrists, but to no avail. These professionals could not cut through my wall of denial.

After two years of this third marriage, my wife conducted a one-person intervention on my alcoholism, which had started at age thirty as I fought to avoid the guilt of my sexaholism. I spent a month at a treatment center, got very active in AA, and have not had a drink since then. But I didn't get well!

In fact, I got a lot worse. Without alcohol to mask my guilt, I had to face my sexual addiction alone. A number of suicidal episodes ensued, and I was hospitalized twice for extreme depression. Eventually my wife confronted me over my sexaholism, and I started to attend SA meetings on a regular basis. At the time I felt that the program wasn't right for me. It didn't work, and I didn't stay sober. I wasn't ready for the program.

Throughout my extreme depression, I had been unable to work. It was almost impossible for me to get out of bed most of the time, and I was certified for long-term disability benefits. No one knew whether I would ever be able to work again.

After two years of deep depression, the loss of my professional career, and the end of insurance, I was forced to change psychiatrists. This new professional decided very quickly that I was manic-depressive and needed medication for that condition. His diagnosis, based on the ups and downs of my addictive cycle, was wrong, but the medication did level out my life to the point where I felt I could get some kind of job. As I searched for work, it seemed that everyone felt that I was over-qualified for any job I thought I could handle. After several months, I decided to go to California for a fresh start.

Arriving in California, I soon found routine nonprofessional work by not disclosing my education or work history. Although I attended AA meetings with some regularity, I didn't make any SA contacts there. I drifted steadily into pornography, porno shops, and porno flicks.

Eventually my third wife gave up all hope of helping me. I found myself living alone in a flop-house hotel, frequenting the porno places, losing my job, and really going crazy. Desperation drove me once again to the brink of suicide.

Hopeless, in this darkest night of my soul, I looked up the SA number and phoned for help. I got to an SA meeting, got a sponsor right away, worked the Steps diligently, stayed sober, and got to Step Nine within a few months.

With one year of sobriety, and a lot of work on Steps Nine, Ten, and Eleven, I returned to the Southwest, and to my second wife and family. After a second year of sobriety and total abstinence, we remarried. I have continued to go to SA meetings and to work the Steps. I do extensive Twelfth Step work with prisoners. Life has never been better.

Sober since 1988, I have been relieved from obsession and compulsion. My spiritual development has been enhanced through prayer and meditation, through a steady diet of spiritual reading, and through the inspiration of several very caring and inspiring ministers.

Every aspect of my life has changed. Love has replaced lust to a very great extent. The mere avoidance of acting out has been replaced largely by a more positive sobriety and the actions of love. While my first wife is deceased, I enjoy a good friendship with my third wife. And I am pursuing healing relationships with my nine children, twenty-four grandchildren, and three great-grandchildren. If I live long enough, I am determined to have them know and love the new father, grandfather, and great-grandfather they have never known.

There are a number of lessons that I have learned at various stages of my recovery:

> When I lived alone in my first year of sobriety, I learned that life without sex is infinitely better than life with compulsive sex.

> When I lived with my second wife for a year before we remarried, I learned that love without sex is infinitely better than sex without love.

Since our remarriage, I have learned that making love is infinitely better than having sex.

In recovery, I continue to be surprised that there are no limits to the development of positive sobriety, spiritual life, and love in action.

Through telling parts of my story and sharing my experience, strength, and hope with prisoners in some five hundred letters over the last ten years, I have observed that the more I give to others, the more comes back to me.

My life is manageable today, but I have to remember who the manager is. God is truly doing for me what I could not do for myself. I have experienced all of the promises of the program to a very significant degree.

I continue to work the SA program on a daily basis. I attend meetings regularly. I continue to make amends as opportunities occur. I take inventory continuously and try to correct my thoughts, words, and actions in midstream. I pray and meditate daily, and continue to discover and pursue God's will for me. I continue to serve as a local SA contact, to sponsor those who ask, and to sponsor prisoners by mail.

I thank God every day for my new life, my growing ability to love, and SA.

33. Grow Old with Me

I had to face the fact that in my marriage I didn't know what intimacy without sex looked like. I was always seeking to create intimacy so I could get my wife to have sex with me—just like I did with the girlfriends who preceded her. Our sexual encounters usually came out of the "connect with me and make me whole" syndrome. They created a false intimacy that soon evaporated, often leaving exposed the underlying emotions that made us feel that we had to be sexual with each other in the first place. I was usually left with a craving for more.

That is why I began to look for progressive victory over lust in my marriage. I wanted to learn how to relate to my wife as a friend and partner-in-life. I chose to practice abstinence because of what I hoped it would do for me. My wife gave me the space to do this—reluctantly at first. I really didn't give her the option. Even back then I sensed that as long as I was depending on her to fill my sexual needs, I was not going to find the kind of sobriety I need and want. My wife could never fill the sexual void that had driven me to look for satisfaction outside our marriage.

After two years of abstinence, my wife and I went away for a long weekend and had plenty of sex. I got really high on it. I figured this was okay because it was with my wife. It seemed right to celebrate after such a long dry spell, but I came away from the holiday wondering how often we could have this sort of encounter without me losing my sobriety.

My wife commented that in only a month's time we could be sexual with each other again because the kids would be staying with friends. This raised my expectations. I marked the weekend on the calendar in my mind and began ticking off the days, one by one. When the night finally arrived, we got into a disagreement over dinner. Sex was the last thing on her mind and the only thing on mine! I was so angry when she rebuffed my attempts to initiate contact that I couldn't sleep. She owed me sex. She'd promised. I tossed and turned all night.

I felt like a little boy whose mother had pulled the chocolate chip cookie right out of his hand when he was about to take a big bite. The next day I gave my wife the silent, withdrawn, "I'm-really-angry-at-you" treatment. I knew I couldn't go on living like this. If this was sobriety, I had to find something better or sobriety wouldn't last.

As a married sexaholic, I had thought that I could still get my fix, legitimately. Once I decided to start giving up lust in my marriage by practicing prolonged periods of abstinence, I went through withdrawal similar to my experience when I stopped masturbating. I found myself craving sex with my wife, making suggestive comments, and being physically affectionate with the hope she would respond sexually. I did things that would make her happy in the hope that sex would be my reward.

I consulted with some members who were further down the road of recovery from lust in their marriages and found that some of them were letting their wives take the initiative with regard to sex. Now that was a threatening thought! But the more I pondered it, the more sense it made. It was another way of surrendering to my Higher Power and giving up my attempt to control my wife.

Several years later, after more prolonged periods of sexual abstinence, my wife suggested we might have sex one night if I came home from my SA meeting early. By then, I had learned that if I allowed myself to have any expectations of sex and they went unfulfilled, I was asking for trouble. So I thought, I'm not coming home from my meeting early. I'll go to fellowship and then come home. If she wants sex when I get home, that will be fine. If not, I'm not going to build up any self-centered expectations.

When I arrived home from my meeting, my wife apologized for leading me to believe that we might have sex. She was too tired and wanted to call it a night. I was able to reply honestly that I was okay with that. What a contrast to the previous incident where I had spent the whole night and the following day consumed by resentment fueled by my thwarted lustful desires! I was finally learning that I need God more than sex, and freedom more than pleasure in my marriage.

Now the initiative to practice abstinence in our marriage started to come from my wife. At one point she said to me, "You know, there are a lot of ways we can express physical intimacy toward each other without it leading to sex." I thought, "Oh, really?" In my sexaholic mind, I tended to sexualize all physical expressions of intimacy.

I began to accept that I was captive to the pleasure I got from sex in our marriage. I could see that our sexual involvement with each other often did not have that much to do with genuine intimacy. There was nothing wrong with the pleasure our sexual relations gave me. The problem lay in my inability to take it or leave it. Once I said yes to sex, even after being sexually abstinent for prolonged periods, I had to have it. I craved it. I was compulsive. I had to do it more than once, more than twice, more than three times, until the time or energy ran out. I depended on my wife to set any limit. Was this progressive victory over lust? I decided it wasn't, so I kept returning to sexual abstinence to break the lust cycle that was stunting the growth of our marriage.

Once I became aware that my wife had given up any timetable for sex, I had to ask myself honestly whether or not I even wanted to be married to her. At first the answer was a clear no. What was the point? Over time, the answer became a conditional yes. Now the answer is a positive yes. My wife is sure that I love her whether or not she has sex with me. I am no longer thinking about how long it has been since we had sex or begrudging her the time that has gone by, nor am I wasting time wondering if and when it will happen again.

My wife and I both like the freedom that not using sex as a coping and dependency mechanism has given us. Our extended periods of sexual abstinence have made space for much-needed growth in our marriage. It is amazing how much energy and love we can pour into other relationships and activities now that energy and love aren't being consumed by self-centered sex between us.

I am learning that physical intimacy that is centered in God's love doesn't create the same craving for more that lust does. I know I can live without sex and be happy in my marriage. So does my wife. When we kiss each other, or she puts her hand on my leg when I'm driving, or she affectionately touches me as she passes by in the kitchen, or we give each other a fervent full-body embrace, I know my wife is not thinking she wants to go to bed with me. She's simply saying, "I love you."

Recently we went on vacation for five days without the kids and did not have sex. That's the first time that has ever happened. Previously, we always took advantage of a break like that to have sex—unless we got upset with each other. It felt so healthy to be able to pass it up this time around. It was as if we were finally getting some maturity in our marriage relationship. We had such a good week together working on various projects, going on walks, playing games, sitting by the fire, talking, and expressing physical affection without sexualizing it.

Sober since 1993 and more surrendered than I could have imagined, I like the road I'm on in my marriage. It is not easy, but it is good. I like my increasing freedom from the tyranny of lust and the growing intimacy we are experiencing. We are on a journey together. We know there will always be new insights to gain about the mysteries of being separate individuals joined together in a covenant of marriage made by God.

My wife gave me a magnet that is mounted above my desk along with her picture. It reads, "Grow old with me . . . the best is yet to come." That's exactly what I plan to do, for I believe she is right.

34. Useful after All

I am a middle-aged married woman, and I am a sexaholic.

I wasn't held much as a baby. My mother tells me that I cried whenever I was awake. When I was six months old, my father solved the problem. He conditioned me to stop crying by spanking me. When I started school, I did odd things to get attention, but I got teased instead. I often escaped into my own world, where I could construct fantasies to replace a reality that didn't measure up. I believed that I was going to be famous someday, and everyone would see what a great person I was. I had a lot of fantasies about boys and men. As early as age five, I had crushes on boys. When I saw movies, I focused on romantic images that weren't necessarily even part of the movie. Soon I was spending more time in fantasy than in reality. When I kissed a boy in second grade, the whole class teased us. I began to realize that other people weren't thinking about the same things that I was. My solution was to keep my fantasies to myself.

My IQ scores placed me just below genius, but by sixth grade I was getting failing grades in school. I couldn't face my parents with those grades, so I decided to kill myself. I planned it for a night when my parents were going out. When they returned unexpectedly, I took it as a sign that something in the universe wanted me alive. I did what I thought was necessary to survive—I changed my report card. I felt like a criminal. It was a deliberate turning away from God, but I did it anyway—and it changed me. I felt powerful inside. People sensed the change and stopped teasing me. Through deception, I felt as though I could control my reality.

As I approached puberty, my fantasies became more sexual in nature. I began to involve other kids in them. I did a strip show for one girl and had her do one for me. We hid in the bushes near boys' houses and watched them. Another girl and I pretended to have sex in front of a younger child and upset her terribly. I developed a crush on a little boy that I babysat and fantasized about touching him.

Older boys started giving me the attention I craved. By the age of thirteen I was dating. I felt energized when I started going with a boy, but the feeling wore off quickly as the relationship wore on. As soon as another boy showed an interest, I was off to a new relationship and its accompanying emotional high.

As that pattern continued, my tolerance increased. It was no longer enough to kiss and fantasize. I progressed to heavy petting. I skipped school and forged an absence note. The fear of being caught only heightened the excitement. I finally crossed the line and went all the way at age eighteen. I went away to college and tried to be true to my boyfriend (doing everything except going all the way with seven different men), but within the year I'd had sex with another student and with one of my professors. I told my boyfriend about it, thinking he would probably ask me to marry him, but he dumped me.

My addiction shifted into high gear. I did things I thought I would never do. I discovered masturbation and became so compulsive about it that I wrecked my health, needing an extra year to graduate. I waited tables and played music in bars. I routinely picked up men there. I had sex with two men in one day, and even two men at the same time. I had sex with a bisexual prostitute. I hung out with bikers and lived with drug addicts. I came through a guy's window with a baseball bat. I broke a girl's door down. I had sex with a sixteen-year-old and with a fifty-year-old. I fantasized about sex with men, women, and animals.

I knew that something was wrong. I tried therapy, but ended up having sex with my therapist. I went to a woman therapist, and she prescribed a book of women's pornographic writings. I tried marriage, but that didn't fix me either.

I married a nice man. I never cheated on him, except in my fantasies. I masturbated as a "healthy" outlet. I led the perfect double life. I wasn't acting out; I was acting in. I thought everything was under control, but there was a problem. My husband and I went to basketball games at the local high school. I got bored with the games and began fantasizing about the teenage boys. Later, I would masturbate to sexual fantasies about them.

I even befriended one boy's parents. I fantasized about going for a run with him up into the hills and seducing him. I spent hours perfecting the details of my fantasies. I thought about really asking him if he wanted to go for a jog sometime. He approached me one evening and told me that he was praying for me. (My first thought was, "He likes me!") He continued by explaining that he and his friend prayed for all of the people every day. I realized that he was trying to tell me about his faith. In that moment, I saw myself clearly. I realized that I had become a predator and that my "harmless" fantasies were becoming plans that could harm this boy.

My addiction didn't give up easily. I tried to continue using this boy in my fantasies, but I could no longer masturbate to his image. I realized that my life was going out of control. Even though I hadn't done anything inappropriate on the outside, I knew that on the inside I was no different from people who had. I knew that it was just a matter of time. It was self-preservation that finally brought me to SA. I was forty-four.

I went to an SA information meeting. I was the only woman there, yet as the men told their stories, I could identify with them. I felt like I was at home for the first time in my life. I was a little surprised at the sobriety definition. At that time I didn't understand what masturbation had to do with it, but I was willing to take direction. They assigned me a temporary sponsor and told me to call her. I called her the next day.

She outlined an action plan that seemed excessive. She had me read the AA Big Book, the SA manual, and the *Twelve and Twelve* and listen to Step study tapes as I worked each Step. She gave me Step guides to help me put my thoughts down on paper. I was encouraged to go to as many meetings as possible. The closest meeting was an hour away. On top of that, I was asked to call her every day. After a few days of sobriety, I understood why I needed such a rigorous program when I experienced physical and emotional withdrawal from my addiction.

I kept busy at work during the day, but evenings were difficult. I was jittery and couldn't sleep. I paced the floor. I gained eight pounds during my first month of sobriety because I was overeating to dull the pain. I ran obsessively and damaged my hip so badly that I had to give up running permanently. Painful memories came back as I was writing my First Step. I needed those daily phone calls to my sponsor. I needed the meetings. I needed the "excessive" Step work.

Sobriety became more comfortable gradually. Slowly, I was changing. I became accustomed to staying in reality. An unexpected miracle unfolded. I began to really experience life. It was as though everything had been colorless before and suddenly it was in Technicolor. Until I was sober, I never knew what I was missing.

With sobriety came clarity of mind and a desire to become a better person. I did some research and checked my findings with a psychiatrist. I was diagnosed as having Attention Deficit Disorder and a learning disability. Medication was prescribed that has helped me to do a better job at work. Instead of barely getting the job done, I have been able to contribute significantly to my profession. I have also been able to concentrate well enough to write down the music I hear in my head. The result has been seven publishable arrangements in a year and a half.

The greatest gift in sobriety so far has come through a group of S-Anons. They asked if I was willing to tell my SA story in an S-Anon meeting during a convention. The idea scared me. I didn't think that they would be very sympathetic. After all, I was the enemy. But I knew that part of my program was to do things I didn't want to, so I said yes.

The experience made a deep impression on me. As I told my story to the people who had been victimized by people like me, I finally felt the full impact of my actions. I had always known intellectually that my behavior had caused a lot of damage, but I had not felt the loss. Now I felt devastated. I realized that even if I spent the rest of my life trying to make it up to them, I never could make up for the damage that I had caused. In short, I owed them big time. Then this group of people, wounded by people like me, chose to receive me with compassion and forgiveness. As they thanked me for sharing, I felt the responsibility that comes with the gift of this program. It's up to me to stay sober and to carry the message no matter what.

I will always be a sexaholic. I am mentally different from non-sexaholics. If I am willing to make some adjustments, I can continue experiencing the wonderful joy of living in sobriety, free from this compulsion. Here are some adjustments that I have found helpful so far. They may not be for everyone, but they work for me.

> I don't watch TV and movies because I can't handle the images. I have to stay in reality. I haven't been to the beach since I got sober.
>
> I have changed the way I dress to reflect my age and lifestyle.
>
> I go to more than one meeting a week because I need a lot of support to work this "counter-cultural" program.
>
> I write, work, and rework the Twelve Steps. They have become my best friends for dealing with anything that worries or bothers me.
>
> I surrender my will and my life to my Higher Power on a daily basis. I don't run my life or anyone else's any more.
>
> I have a sponsor who has a sponsor who has a sponsor.
>
> I work with newcomers, even the difficult ones who are looking for a lower bottom to hit. They remind me of someone I used to be.

The funny thing is that I *want* to do these things. During all of the years I spent doing whatever felt good, I never felt anywhere near as good as I do now. I finally feel that I am worth something on the inside. It takes a sexaholic to reach a sexaholic, so I carry the message. I am a bent tool that can reach into places other tools cannot. I can be useful after all.

35. Welcome Home

My story is not unique, and for that I am grateful. When I discovered I was a common sexaholic, I became hopeful that my problem had a common solution. Hope and honesty were small words in my vocabulary and an even smaller part of my life before I came to SA.

My grandfathers were alcoholics and possibly sexaholics. My family did not show any visible signs of affection, but today I thank my Higher Power for the strength He gave my folks, as immigrants to America, to make the best life they were able for themselves and their children. I now see how hard that must have been.

That was not always my attitude. I was a demanding and emotionally needy child. I demanded far more than my parents could give, and I grew up feeling deprived. I constantly compared myself to others and was extremely sensitive to and envious of what others got. Theirs was always better. I held that against my parents, and so justified not being part of their lives. I cut myself off and effectively grew up without a family while wallowing in self-pity for the pain I had brought on myself.

I was interested in sexual things from a young age. Today I believe it was part of me from the start. At the age of six I was involved in childhood sexual experimentation with an older neighbor girl. My father caught us and made a big deal of it. While the girl got in trouble, I got the message that we had done something dirty. Around the age of nine I was lured by a thirteen- or fourteen-year-old neighbor boy. There was secrecy and hiding, but his father caught us in the act, and he was beaten with a leather belt. These episodes were shot through with fear of exposure and the excitement of secrecy.

I taught myself masturbation at the age of ten by using an instrument. The event was overwhelming. I became addicted immediately. I knew from past sexual experience that what I was doing was dirty and would get an explosive response from adults. The fear of being caught only heightened the excitement. Dishonesty grew as my secret became harder to protect, and it spawned the double life I led for many years.

I used masturbation to solve all of my problems. As my problems increased, my masturbation increased, at times to the point of physical exhaustion. The toxic effect appeared in my early teens. My fantasies were insufficient. Hard-core pornography was not available then, but there were books with pictures, and masturbation took on new importance. I wanted to act out with all my friends, and I was constantly scheming to see them and touch them sexually.

Voyeurism now became a preoccupation. I would find myself in places like public restrooms for hours on end, bored out of my mind, just to catch a sexual glimpse of a man. The rare times I "got a good look" served to feed my fantasies so I could continue masturbating as my means of coping.

I disconnected from reality and turned so far inward that I really did not know who I was any longer. I latched onto friends and acquaintances, attempting to be with them just to have some kind of identity. My silent demands on them to be everything to me only put me in a position to be hurt. Making these people my gods only made things worse; when I got hurt, it destroyed my trust, which further isolated me, thereby completing the cycle to start the process again.

My need to feel superior supported my belief that I had discovered something unique. Since sex was not discussed at home, I understood only that sex was dirty and forbidden. Yet it brought euphoria and removed me from the world. This solution was short-lived and posed a problem; it had to be repeated endlessly to numb my sense of isolation from God, family, and peers.

I found a beautiful woman whom I loved, and we married. Yet when she turned her attention to her family and our first child, I had the excuse I needed to fulfill my fantasies by acting out with men. Pornography shops were just opening, and hard-core films were being shown. My first movie was like a bomb exploding in my head. I was changed forever. My innocence was completely gone. My fantasies became more intense, and my addiction deepened. Dishonesty put down new roots as I took advantage of my employer's trust in me and took time from my job to act out. I lied to my family, using a side business activity as an excuse for my late returns home.

My ignorance of street life got me an intense infestation of crab lice. When I found out what they were, I had a bout with shame, embarrassment and self loathing the likes of which I had never known. Even worse, it affected my marriage because I passed the infestation to my wife. This brought shock and overwhelming fear, fear that I was involving an innocent person in my perverse behavior, fear that I might bring her something more serious—but most of all fear that I would be found out. I said nothing and left her to figure out what to do and decided to cease all sexual activity with her.

I visited the new porno shops, spending the family money on books and movies, and bomb after bomb exploded in my head. I learned about bath houses, which I perceived as an endless supply of lust objects. At last my fantasies could be realized, and I didn't need my wife and family any more. But, as before, the toxic effect appeared. I needed more and more, yet felt less and less satisfied. I began to perceive that something was dreadfully wrong.

My solution was simple: go to a therapist, place my money on the table, and sit back and relax while I got fixed. Over a ten-year period, I went through seven therapists and three priests, all of whom practically begged me to stop acting out so I could get to the issues at hand. Each week brought the same story until they got frustrated and let me go. I even suggested to them that I was addicted and needed something like AA, but my quest for the easier, softer way blinded me to the true solution, even as it was at my doorstop.

The addiction escalated. I took more risks with my personal safety and that of my family by paying for sex and bringing strangers home. I also played roulette with the deadly disease AIDS. By now the dishonesty was rampant as my double life expanded. I presented myself to the world as a moral, righteous person, while engaging in a secret life of shameful, immoral behavior. The guilt was crushing, the pain was intense, and the energy spent was enormous. I always believed in God, but my faulty thinking kept me separated from God. I knew in my sick mind that God would never come to the filthy places I visited.

My sexaholism progressed to the point where my whole life caved in on me in a church one afternoon. Leaving my workplace at lunchtime, I thought about turning left toward a porn parlor, where I could spend the hour acting out, or turning right toward a nearby cathedral, where there was a noon hour service. I turned right. I sat through the service, feeling like a moral leper and scarcely participating. Afterward, as the church emptied and the lights were quenched, I remained in my pew. I couldn't have told you at the time why I turned right and walked to the cathedral or why I remained there, but now I believe that both impulses came from God. Sitting alone in the now-dark church, I was suddenly hit by the realization that nothing I was doing made a difference and that I was doomed to a life of acting out. I was going to lose everything and possibly die. I broke down and cried bitter tears of powerlessness like I'd never felt before. I realized I could not purge this from my life. Then came the sinking feeling that no one else could purge it either, not even God. I now see that as a First Step experience for me, but I was condemned to terrible hopelessness for four more years because I had not yet come to believe; I didn't have the Second Step. My acting out continued, the disease progressed, and the pain and guilt became ever more intense. The solution, I then decided, was to take a drug to kill my sexual appetite for a time, to try to live life without lust and sex.

As God ordered things, two days before my first injection someone with whom I had acted out in a porno shop and who shared my problem became my connection to SA. I read that wonderful SA brochure and cried again, this time with tears of hope. I was excited about going to my first meeting, but feared that I would find a den of lust. Instead, as I told my story, they heard my desperation and they said the golden words to me that I shall always treasure, "Welcome home." It was then that I realized how lost I was, and it was then that I took Step Two. God came to me and I knew it.

Step Three was not yet for me because I had to test my solutions once more. After two and a half months, I acted out one more time. It was then that I realized I would lose my last hope if I didn't become honest and turn my whole life and will over to God. That was 1985. I thank God for the willingness to make that decision, for without it there would be no program, and what I wanted most, sexual sobriety, would have been nothing more than wishful thinking.

I see today how far God has brought me. Steps Four through Twelve have shown me how much humility I must have to stay sober and what a long way I must journey in recovery, one day at a time. This gives me peace because my life today has purpose and direction. The awesome power of God through this program has restored in me an innocence my sexual addiction had taken from me.

I continued to abstain from sex with my wife, the abstinence prompted by my lice infestation, well into my years of sobriety. After seventeen years, I was ready to resume relations. But my wife wasn't. This woman, my beautiful bride, continued the abstinence for a total of twenty-seven years. Then one evening, the period of abstinence surprisingly and miraculously ended for us, showing us that God was doing for us what we could not do for ourselves.

The Promises (*AA* 83-84) are coming true for me today, and I cling to my Higher Power as tightly as I am able, for I have been shown that without this life-saving program I have no God, and without God I have nothing.